CAMBRIDGE

MEMORIES OF TIMES PAST

HINC LUCEM ET POCULA SACRA

77 PAINTINGS BY WILLIAM MATTHISON

INTRODUCTION BY MIKE PETTY
TEXT BY SARAH WOODALL AND COLIN INMAN

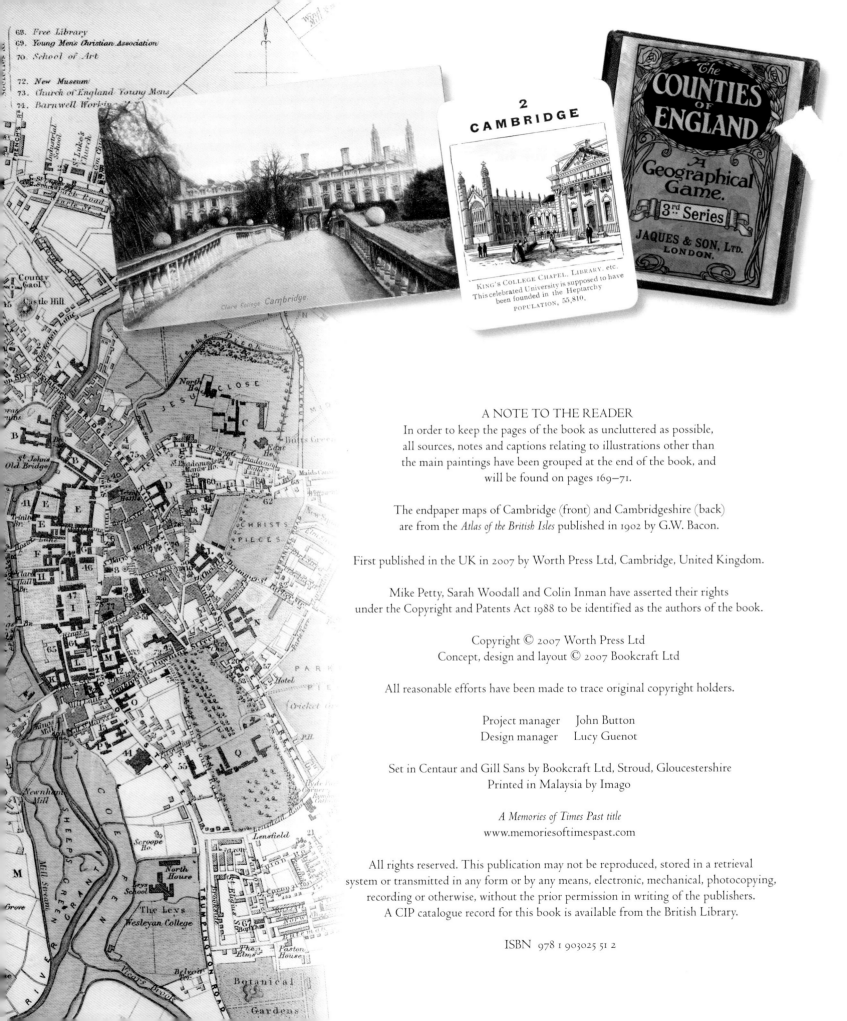

A NOTE TO THE READER

In order to keep the pages of the book as uncluttered as possible, all sources, notes and captions relating to illustrations other than the main paintings have been grouped at the end of the book, and will be found on pages 169–71.

The endpaper maps of Cambridge (front) and Cambridgeshire (back) are from the *Atlas of the British Isles* published in 1902 by G.W. Bacon.

First published in the UK in 2007 by Worth Press Ltd, Cambridge, United Kingdom.

Mike Petty, Sarah Woodall and Colin Inman have asserted their rights under the Copyright and Patents Act 1988 to be identified as the authors of the book.

Copyright © 2007 Worth Press Ltd
Concept, design and layout © 2007 Bookcraft Ltd

All reasonable efforts have been made to trace original copyright holders.

Project manager   John Button
Design manager   Lucy Guenot

Set in Centaur and Gill Sans by Bookcraft Ltd, Stroud, Gloucestershire
Printed in Malaysia by Imago

A Memories of Times Past title
www.memoriesoftimespast.com

ISBN   978 1 903025 51 2

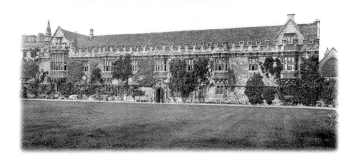

CONTENTS

BACON'S
LARGE SCALE
PLAN
OF
CAMBRIDGE

Cloth Case, 6d.
On Cloth, 1s.

THE ROVER CYCLES

FROM THE ORDNANCE SURVEY

G. W. BACON & CO., Ltd., 127, STRAND, LONDON.

CAMB

Described by N.
Pictured by E. W

THE GREAT COURT, TRINITY COLLEGE

BLACKIE

CAMBRIDGE 1907

MIKE PETTY

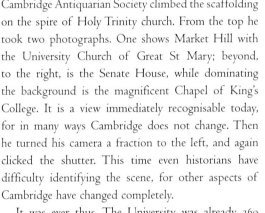

At the start of the Edwardian era a member of the Cambridge Antiquarian Society climbed the scaffolding on the spire of Holy Trinity church. From the top he took two photographs. One shows Market Hill with the University Church of Great St Mary; beyond, to the right, is the Senate House, while dominating the background is the magnificent Chapel of King's College. It is a view immediately recognisable today, for in many ways Cambridge does not change. Then he turned his camera a fraction to the left, and again clicked the shutter. This time even historians have difficulty identifying the scene, for other aspects of Cambridge have changed completely.

It was ever thus. The University was already 260 years old when Elizabeth I visited Cambridge in 1564. She came to view the chapel that had recently been completed by her father, Henry VIII. Nearby she found the new colleges of Christ's, St John's, Magdalene and Trinity that had grown on the site of the religious houses he had dissolved. Emmanuel would follow twenty years later, Sidney Sussex ten years after that.

It was largely unchanged when Queen Victoria visited Cambridge in 1847 to witness her beloved husband, Albert, being installed as Chancellor of the University. Doctors, lawyers and priests were learning their skills in an ancient foundation, which still demanded both Latin and Greek from its undergraduates. Yet by her death, Cambridge had been transformed. Hundreds of new houses had sprung up in the surrounding fields, and the University's Botanic Garden had been moved from the town centre. In its place were new scientific departments, with research at the Cavendish Laboratory attracting international attention.

Cambridge 1902 Coronation Medal (top left); advertisement and cover from *Spalding's Condensed Guide to Cambridge*, 1906; The Bridge of Sighs, an 1896 photochrome (top right); the 1902 photograph referred to in the text; and a 1907 gold sovereign – £1 notes did not appear until 1914.

Newnham College, a 1908 "real photograph" postcard (above); King Edward VII at his Coronation, from *Edward VII: His Life and Times*, 1910 (below).

In another development just as radical, two women's colleges had been established. Mildred Tuker, the author of the volume about Cambridge from which the paintings in this volume are taken, had attended one of these, Newnham. In her 1907 book she recounted the history of the University, which had grown to dominate the ancient riverside town where it had sought sanctuary in the thirteenth century. Its magnificent architecture had transformed the mean town streets. Its colleges provided employment to the population who served it, town tradesmen were licenced to trade with university students, and town shops shut when the University went down at the end of term.

At the same time Eglantyne Jebb, a well-to-do young lady who worked for the Charity Organisation Society in Cambridge and later became co-founder of the Save the Children Fund, was surveying another Cambridge, the one the academics seldom glimpsed. It was a town whose residents were grappling with problems of poverty and unemployment, overcrowding and homelessness, issues that national government was just beginning to address.

The Cambridge that entered the twentieth century was undergoing dramatic change. New houses had been built, but with few facilities such as schools and churches. There was now, however, more co-operation between town and gown, with the University giving up many of its powers over civic affairs and electing its own members to the Borough Council.

The two communities walked the same streets but they never mixed. They spoke the same language but could not communicate with each other. They had nothing in common except the town in which they lived

and worked. Famous academics, whose names were spoken of in educated households around the world, would not be recognised outside their colleges, where they had everything they needed for their research and teaching. There was, however, one group of people who could experience both Cambridges. They were the college porters who guarded the gates, welcomed their members past and present, and in the evening retired to their small college-owned terraced house in a town backstreet.

THE NEW KING

In 1901 town and gown together mourned their Queen and prepared to proclaim her successor. The University's announcement of the new King Edward VII was made inside the Senate House, then repeated to the crowds gathered outside. Next day came the official proclamations by both the town and county of Cambridge. They were made on different days because of administrative confusion. It had, of course, been many years since such a ceremony had been performed, but the Edwardian era seemed to have two of everything.

The new King was a Cambridge man. In 1861, when Prince of Wales, he had been enrolled as a member of Trinity College, though he was to live out at Madingley Hall away from the possibly corrupting influences of other undergraduates. The newspapers were soon full of stories of his exploits on the hunting field, and how he had fallen into the river whilst rowing. He became attracted to an Irish actress, provoking a scandal that required his father Albert to travel down to Madingley to remonstrate with his errant son. In 1883 Edward saw his own son, Prince Albert Victor, follow in his footsteps to Trinity College. The young prince also copied his father's other interests; in 1885 it was Edward who had to journey to Cambridge to remonstrate with an erring son over an escapade with an actress.

Months of planning, debates and discussion took place to decide a suitable way of marking Edward's

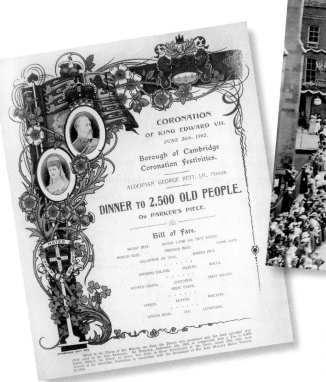

Coronation. Organisers planned a meal on Parker's Piece for those Cambridge folk who had been present at the coronation celebrations of Queen Victoria in 1838. Then 15,000 had been entertained to a meal on Parker's Piece; this time some 2,500 people would be fed under the shelter of marquees. The aged poor had to be identified, located, equipped with knife, fork and spoon, and transported to the Piece for their outdoor dinner. Try as they might, however, the Council could find only 250 residents qualified to attend.

As the great day neared there came an alarming announcement: the King was seriously ill and needed an operation. The Coronation would have to be postponed. Amidst fears for His Majesty's health came the realisation that all the events planned would have to be cancelled too. But there was a major problem – the food for the old folks' meal was already in the ovens. Cooks from Trinity College and Trinity Hall had already baked 68 large meat pies and 58 gooseberry and cherry tarts. What were they to do with them?

It was agreed that rather than waste it the food should be distributed to its intended recipients to eat in their own homes. The *Cambridge Daily News* reported: "Several hundred of the poorest inhabitants

of Cambridge gathered outside the Corn Exchange when the distribution began. Along all the streets those who had come for a share of the good things hastened towards the entrance as quickly as their too-evident infirmities would allow them. The halt, the lame and the blind were there. Some hobbled along on crutches, others moved slowly with the aid of sticks. Baskets, bags and all manner of receptacles had been brought. Quite a number who had come empty-handed wrapped up quantities of fruit tarts in newspapers – grimy newspapers – that could hardly have improved the semi-liquid contents."

The postponement was a short one, and on 9 August the Corporation and dignitaries proceeded to King's College Chapel for the celebration service. Street after street was bright with flags blazing in a brave show of scarlet and white and blue. Visitors poured in by road and rail, in vehicles and on foot, until it seemed as though the whole population of Cambridgeshire must have drifted en masse into the town and left the surrounding countryside empty and desolate. There was a parade of decorated

The Coronation Dinner invitation from 1902 (top left); the Cambridge Coronation Procession in a contemporary photograph (above); the reverse of the Coronation Medal shown on page 1 (above); Edward VII being crowned, from a *Coronation Souvenir* produced "with the compliments of R.W. Righton, Wholesale, Retail and General Draper, Manchester House, Evesham" (below).

The Coronation at Westminster Abbey.

The Coronation Tea Notice, and cakes from *The Book of the Home*, Volume 3 (1905).

A Cambridge motor bus, a "real photograph" postcard of 1907.

vehicles that stretched for a mile and a half, a balloon ascent and promenade concert, culminating with a grand display of fireworks by Messrs Brock. It was an occasion to remember, but the only food was the public luncheon in the Guildhall and that cost 3/6 (18p) a head.

On 4 September even that was put right. Tents sprouted on Parker's Piece, despite the strong winds that tugged tent poles out of the ground. Dozens of women were buttering bread as it fell from a machine, and an engine was heating several boilers each holding 100 gallons of water. Over 800 gallons of tea were brewed, and E.A. Wadsworth provided ginger beer and lemonade. It was consumed by the already well-fed 250 old folk who were joined by 6,000 children rounded up from all the schools in the Borough and the Mayor distributed Coronation Medals.

GETTING AROUND

At the turn of the twentieth century, public transport in Cambridge was provided by horse-drawn trams in competition with horse-drawn buses. In 1902 news broke that the Omnibus Company was to be wound up. The buses would be seriously missed, as many employees in shops and offices now lived so far out of town that without them it would be a problem to get to and from their homes in the hour usually allowed

for dinner. The Company's vehicles were auctioned at their stables in Chesterton Road in November 1902. A two-horse omnibus fitted with garden seats on the top sold for 20 guineas, others went for just £4 10s.

This left the roads clear for the Cambridge Street Tramway Company. It had been established in 1880 with lines from the station to Market Hill, St Andrews Street and East Road. They were generally considered much too slow. The future was believed to be electric power – no smelly piles of horse droppings, no motor fumes – and there was already an electricity generating station on Quayside which could supply the current. A new Cambridge Electric Tramways Syndicate had plans for expansion to the outlying areas, but proposals for central routes were opposed because of the narrowness of the streets. Before anything could happen they had to purchase the existing lines owned by the Street Tramway Company, who held out for a very high price. As a result the whole scheme foundered.

In 1905 motor buses arrived. Two companies were established, one painted in the light blue of Cambridge, the other in the darker shade of Oxford. The buses were driven by petrol, had non-slipping tyres, and were upholstered with spring cushions inside and seats like light garden chairs outside. Within a week a Cambridge cartoonist depicted one of the buses plunging along at a terrific rate, much to the alarm of a female passenger, who has thrown her arms around the driver's neck to ensure her safety. Simultaneously the bus has struck a lamppost and run over a dog.

From the open-top upper decks, passengers could look into student's rooms, and the buses filled the streets with fumes, both of which fuelled opposition. Within a year both companies' vehicles had been banned and the old horse trams, now renovated and repainted, reigned supreme. It was not to last. In 1907 J.B. Walford introduced his Ortona motor buses, and competition resumed. This time the trams could not survive. They continued until February 1914 when the trams made their last runs, packed with hundreds of

passengers anxious to say they had travelled on such relics of a bygone age.

Buses were a danger to bicycles – though cyclists were as often a danger to themselves. The police courts were busy convicting offenders, both town, undergraduate and more senior members of the University. In 1904 Professor Darwin (son of Charles Darwin, the naturalist) was summonsed for riding a bicycle on the footpath on Coe Fen and fined five shillings.

But the greatest danger was motor cars. The first car in Cambridge had been driven by an undergraduate, Charles Rolls (who was later to team up with a Mr Royce to produce his own vehicles) in 1897. Cars soon caught on. By 1905 the *Cambridge Daily News* commented "It is doubtful if any town the size of Cambridge has as many motors and motor-cycles running about the streets as are to be seen in term time. All day long the 'pouf-pouf' of panting engines is to be heard in our streets and we are becoming quite accustomed to

having an undergraduate motorist fly by within a foot of one's elbows. Some are expert drivers, some are not, but there is no class determined to get more pace out of his machine."

It was the speed that was the problem. In February 1907 a Chinese undergraduate of St Catharine's College was summonsed for driving a motor car in Jesus Lane at a furious rate. Frederick Siggers, a college porter, said he was wheeling a plate basket when the car passed within two feet of the wall on the wrong side of the road at 18 miles an hour. The student said it would be a wonderful car that could get up to that speed after a sharp corner. He was, however, convicted and his licence endorsed. In 1908 the University forbade undergraduates from keeping motor cars without permission.

ENTERTAINMENTS FOR ALL

It needed little excuse for undergraduates to organise a "rag", a key ingredient of which was a bonfire on Market Hill, on which market stalls, shutters and anything else combustible would be burnt. Guy Fawkes' night was a regular flashpoint, but there were many others. In 1902 the declaration of peace in South Africa resulted in a fierce contest between the police and the united forces of town and gown, leading to the widespread destruction of property. In King Street a large double gate was attacked as wood for a bonfire, but a vigorous-looking dame appeared from the other side. Her only weapon was a duster, but such a formidable appearance did she present that the crowd melted away before her advance. University proctors and town police struggled to maintain order with battles around the police station in St Andrew's Street that had opened on the site of

The Last Tram, East Road, 1910, from a contemporary postcard (top left); postcards from 1905 by the cartoonists Harry Moden and Frank Keene (left and below).

Arthur Conan Doyle in 1904, and the New Theatre programme for Sherlock Holmes.

An Oriental Booklover by Olle Hjörtzberg, from *Penrose's Pictorial Annual 1907–8* (left); Mike's source needed (right)

the infamous '"Spinning House", the University's gaol for prostitutes.

Opposite stood the New Theatre, where crowds flocked to see a play based on one of Conan Doyle's adventures of Sherlock Holmes, whose failure to locate "The Missing Three-Quarter" – a Cambridge undergraduate who had disappeared on the eve of the Varsity rugger match – had been published in 1904.

Performances were often interrupted by undergraduates. One young man was ejected on three occasions in one week, prompting his college, St John's, to have him "sent down" from the University. This was the excuse for an elaborate "mock funeral" – a procession of thirteen cabs filled with "mourners" and musicians, which filed along the streets at funeral pace conveying the "corpse" to the railway station and his train home. The cortege halted outside the New Theatre to allow the gathering to indicate its disapproval of the management.

Some student stunts have passed into Cambridge history. In March 1905 the Mayor, Alderman Spalding, received a telegram to say that the Sultan of Zanzibar would be arriving at the station in two hours' time and would appreciate an escort around the ancient town and its colleges. He despatched a carriage to meet the visitors – he had his suspicions, and sent not the official Mayor's coach, but the omnibus from the Lion Hotel with one of the hotel waiters as escort. The royal party in turbans and flowing white robes descended in majesty from the train, and the entourage was escorted

to a bazaar in the Guildhall (the stallholders were disappointed that they spent not a halfpenny), thence to King's, Caius and Trinity, where a prince fell to his knees praising its architecture in a language that none (including the interpreter) understood. After three-quarters of an hour it was time for the visitors to depart, and with many salaams they set off for the station. Crowds who had gathered to watch learned something more of the mysterious ways of the orient when the royal party suddenly dashed to a couple of hansom cabs and disappeared at speed towards Hills Road. The next evening a representative from the *Daily Mail* travelled to Cambridge with "exclusive" news – it had all been a marvellous undergraduate hoax by members of Trinity College headed by William Horace de Vere Cole, who was to go on to establish a reputation as the "Prince of Practical Jokers".

VARSITY AFFAIRS

The Zanzibar hoax was perpetrated at a time when Cambridge was full of dignitaries for an important vote on whether Greek should remain a compulsory subject in the University curriculum. Masters of Arts from all parts of England poured in by rail and road, trams and cabs did a roaring trade, foot passengers thronged the narrow thoroughfares, and motor cars dodged in and out of the traffic. When the Prime Minister, Mr Balfour, arrived at the Senate House to record his vote he was given a rousing reception. The outcome was heralded by a burst of cheering – Greek was triumphant and would continue to be an essential part of University life.

But another tradition was soon to be lost. The highlight of the academic year was the announcement of the Senior Wrangler, the man with the highest marks in the Mathematical Tripos. Within a few minutes the name of the winner was telegraphed to the furthest corners of the earth and published in newspapers as far afield as India, South Africa and New Zealand. There were celebrations too at the other

end of the academic spectrum. Towards the end of the presentation ceremony, in the solemnity of the Senate House, the man with the lowest marks was presented with a large wooden spoon emblazoned and trimmed with his college colours, which was lowered down from the gallery by his friends. In 1906 the University agreed proposals to restructure the Mathematical Tripos, and the last wooden spoon was awarded in 1909.

Further proof that the University was changing came when, in 1904, Edward VII and Queen Alexandra opened the new Sedgwick Museum, the Squire Law Library, and the Botanical and Medical Schools in Downing Street. The same year Cambridge hosted the meeting of the British Association for the Advancement of Science, while Nobel prizes were awarded for work at the Cavendish Laboratory in 1904, 1906 and 1908. But the University would still not admit women to full academic status. Although Cambridge had two women's colleges, Girton and Newnham, whose ladies were allowed to attend lectures and even sit examinations, they were not awarded degrees. The matter had been put to a vote in 1897 when the proposal was overwhelmingly rejected.

In 1907 the most important woman in a male undergraduate's life was his bedmaker. She was an institution, and without her student life would be almost unimaginable. A good "Bedder" was a surrogate mother, and stood up staunchly for her "young gentlemen" in his hour of need. The male equivalent of the "Bedder" was the "Gyp" – Greek for "vulture" – who enjoyed a reputation for making as much money as possible out of his young ward. It was important for an undergraduate to look the part, and there were many Cambridge tailors and robemakers eager to make the acquaintance of new students. Yet as the *Cambridge Daily News* complained in February 1906, the old standards were starting to slip: "Modern undergraduates' dress is a neat disorder. Flannel trousers, brogues, a fancy waistcoat, a shooting jacket and low golfing collar is the costume in which he lounges into his lectures or goes to the theatre in the evening."

Cambridge tradesmen often had problems getting their money from undergraduates, whose idea of economy consisted in owing rather than paying. Messrs Nichols & Sons, grocers, sued one undergraduate over the sum of £5 2s for cherry jam and Scotch whisky, tinned herrings and boxes of biscuits. The lad was under age, and his father refused to pay, claiming that he had told his son not to run into debt and was already providing him with an allowance of £200 a year. In 1906 Mrs Moyes of the Lion

The Order of The Wooden Spoon, *The London Magazine*, Volume 8 (1907) (top left); Squire Law School and Library, from Jarrold's *Pictures in Colour of Cambridge*, 1913 (top right); three postcards from 1905 by the cartoonists Harry Moden and Frank Keene (right)

One of Lance Thackeray's "Lighter Side of the Varsity" images produced for Raphael Tuck's "Oilette" postcards in 1906 (left); "At the Pike and Eel after the Races", a postcard from 1910 (right).

May Week, a 1905 postcard (left); "After the Theatre", a colour photograph from *Penrose's Pictorial Annual 1911–12* (right).

Hotel unsuccessfully claimed payment from an undergraduate for the hire of three horses on the same day – he had tossed up with two friends and lost. The lad, who had recently gone up to Trinity College, found himself associating with men of wealth reputed to dine on larks on toast, turtle soup, snipe and saddle of lamb, using silver cutlery brought from home.

By the time May Week came around, the highlight of the Cambridge year when the town was filled with young ladies anxious to join their beaux in celebrating the end of the academic year, everyone's finances were severely stretched. In 1906 the *Daily News* reported "Cambridge has surrendered to May Week visitors very completely. These pretty butterflies, who transform our mundane streets into kaleidoscope scenes of colour and animation, mean increased profit for the tradesman and are a source of joy to the lodging-house keeper. They must have somewhere to lay their heads, dainty dinners and mayonnaise for supper." In 1903 May Week coincided with an outbreak of smallpox in which 154 people were infected and 15 died; it was not reported until after the festivities for fear of the detrimental effect it might have.

Much May Week activity revolved around the river. Like Oxford there were "bumping races" between the colleges (the Cam being too narrow for eights to race side by side); the boats started off one behind another, each endeavouring to catch and "bump" the one ahead. After the rowing there was a mass race back to the boatyards, and collisions were frequent.

A LOCAL TRAGEDY

During May Week in 1905, as the *Daily News* had it, "The sinister hand of Death cast its shadow over Cambridge in its most joyous mood." In the midst of the holiday festivities three people were drowned when the ferryboat known as the Red Grind at Fen Ditton capsized. Two journeys had been made after the May Week racing, the ferry being very full each time. As it set off on its third crossing two University men jumped on at the last moment. The ferry lurched and turned turtle, pitching the screaming occupants into six feet of water. Ditton men, hearing the cries, shoved off in their black fishing boats and managed to save all but three of the twenty or so people in the water.

Hundreds of people packed Mill Road for the funeral of one of the young ladies who died in the incident. At that time Mill Road was a part of Cambridge where undergraduates seldom ventured; another was Barnwell, off Newmarket Road, considered a slum area chiefly inhabited by brickmakers. In Barnwell you could pass fourteen alehouses in five minutes. Its residents were proud people, however, as a letter to the *Daily News* testifies: "Sir – Barnwell is not a 'most miserable part of Cambridge' but a neighbourhood inhabited by respectable working people; there are whole streets of bay-windowed respectable residences occupied by shopmen, clerks etc who work in the centre of the town."

Eglantyne Jebb's survey of social conditions in Cambridge in 1906 paints a bleak picture of poverty and unemployment, the town suffering from the wave of depression sweeping over the industrial life of the country. One bright spot was the town's three cement companies which provided work for some 350 men. Cambridge Corporation made arrangements to provide extra work at their stone-breaking yard, and there was employment laying new sewers for the expanding Cherry Hinton area and at the University Botanic Garden, where a Winter Employment Fund supported jobs preparing composts or raking leaves.

END OF AN ERA

It was all a long way from the grassy courts of the college buildings depicted by William Matthison. In 1907 he exhibited a series of paintings of Cambridge scenes that had been commissioned for Mildred Tuker's new book of the same name. His work was praised by the *Daily News*: "His pictures are of a very high order. He has selected the daintiest spots in a town famous for its architectural beauty and many of his pictures represent subjects which are seldom depicted by artists."

That year undergraduates tried to prevent Kier Hardy, the Labour leader, from speaking at the University, but supporters of women's suffrage received backing from the women's colleges. They would receive the vote long before they were allowed to receive Cambridge degrees in 1948. In September Sir John French was at Trinity College making plans for the deployment of thousands of British troops to repel an imaginary enemy landing on the East Anglian coast. Too soon, however, the war would be real, and the carefree times swept away in the carnage of Flanders.

The Edwardian era was nearly over. At 11.50 pm on 6 May 1910 the formal announcement was made from Buckingham Palace that the King had breathed his last. His final illness had followed a chill caught during a flying visit to Sandringham – to some in Cambridge a reminder that his father, Prince Albert, had died of typhoid fever following a chill caught during that winter journey to remonstrate with his student son at Madingley.

King George V was formally proclaimed by the Vice Chancellor in the Senate House at 11 am on 10 May 1910. The officials then emerged on the steps of the Senate House where trumpeters in pale blue uniforms tentatively sounded a fanfare, and the proclamation was made once more by the Deputy Registrar. The ceremony was repeated by both town and county, this time on the same day.

King Edward VII's Lying-in-State, 16–19 May 1910, from *Edward VII: His Life and Times* (above); Cambridge cement works, from an unsigned original painting of c.1911 (left).

WILLIAM MATTHISON

1883–1923

COLIN INMAN

William Matthison was born in Harborne, then in Staffordshire and now part of Birmingham, in 1853, the son of a house agent. He was educated at King Edward's School in Birmingham and when he was fifteen attended drawing classes at Birmingham's Central School of Art and studied under the artist Edward Watson. He also joined the Clarendon Art Fellowship, a group of artists who painted together in the Midlands countryside.

Keble College from the Parks, from Robert Peel and H.C. Minchin's *Oxford*, 1905.

He painted in the Cotswolds in 1874, and by 1875 had decided to become a professional artist. He sketched scenes in south Warwickshire in 1877 and settled in the village of Tysoe. In August 1878 he married Mary Hannah Fessy – the name is spelt Fessy and Fessey in different sources – at Shipston on Stour. In 1881 he and his wife, with their baby Kate Pauline, were living in the village of Tysoe with Mary's mother. The census describes him as "artist landscape painter".

In 1883 they moved to Broughton Road, Banbury, in Oxfordshire. He had to take in private pupils to supplement his income, but he spent the summer holidays painting elsewhere, particularly around Whitby in Yorkshire. By 1891 Matthison had moved to 2 Dashwood Terrace, Neithrop; they were still there in 1901. Matthison's studio was at the same address.

Since he had to travel to Oxford several times a week to give lessons, they moved again in 1902 to Park Town in Oxford. There he was commissioned by the Robert Peel Postcard Company to paint 70 views of the university and city. These were sold by E. Cross of Pembroke Street at seven for a shilling (5p). When Robert Peel gave up producing postcards in 1910, the plates of the Oxford postcards were sold to Alden & Co., who continued to sell them and published in 1912 a book, *Fifty Watercolour Drawings of Oxford*, for the most part consisting of his pictures.

Matthison also received commissions to paint scenes of London and Cambridge for postcards produced by

Raphael Tuck & Sons; and in 1905 he produced a set of six postcards of Thames steamers operated by Salter Brothers.

The commission from A&C Black for 60 to 75 illustrations for *Cambridge* came in 1904. In fact he produced 77 paintings for the book. An exhibition of 63 of the illustrations from *Cambridge* was held at Heffer & Sons to coincide with publication of the book. The *Cambridge Daily News* reviewer regarded Matthison as having "selected the daintiest spots in a town famous for its architectural beauty ... His style is not cramped or mechanically precise, and while true to detail, he exhibits a freedom of expression which is refreshing. As a rule the pictures are bright and fresh in colour; but there are exceptions in which the colour appears too aggressive".

Twenty-four of the illustrations from *Cambridge* were published in four sets of six postcards by Tuck, though, surprisingly, none were issued by A&C Black themselves.

In 1911 there was an exhibition in Oxford of 95 of Matthison's paintings, and one reviewer wrote: "Mr Matthison's work is full of sunshine and colour. Even the rain in St Giles or the High Street does not depress him: he sees it through rose-coloured spectacles, and paints it so we can see it too. His mists are never a hopeless grey, they have a rosy lining." This is a suggestion that his paintings had a "chocolate box" quality. He was not the first of A&C Black's artists to be accused of this, and there is some evidence that the publisher preferred pictures "with bright colouring". Matthison's paintings for *Cambridge* would have met this requirement admirably.

In 1915 the Matthisons moved to Headington to rent a smaller house in Old High Street, then numbered 2 but now renumbered 4. Their only daughter Kate married Wilfrid Evans in the autumn of that year. Matthison continued to accept commissions while living there, including paintings for Lady Rhondda of Llanwern Park.

After the First World War they moved again, this time to a newly built house in High Street, Old Headington (today 12 Old High Street). Matthison died at Park Lea, Headington, on 25 January 1926 at the age of 71. He was buried in Headington Cemetery. Mary Hannah survived him by thirteen years and died at the age of 91.

Information about Matthison can be found on the excellent Headington website at www.headington.org. uk. Sadly, no photograph of the artist appears to have survived.

The Lake, Worcester Gardens, Oxford, from Robert Peel and H.C. Minchin's *Oxford*, 1905.

PLATE 1

THE BRIDGE OF SIGHS, ST JOHN'S COLLEGE

Cambridge's most famous bridge – "so pretty and picturesque" in Queen Victoria's opinion –
connects the two halves of St John's College.

A new bridge over the Cam became necessary in the early nineteenth century to provide access to New Court, the first part of St John's to be built on the west bank of the river. The style of the court is Gothic Revival – not a faithful imitation of medieval architecture but a romantic reinterpretation of it – and the bridge is in keeping with that.

The choice of a name for this bridge was also a romantic notion: it alludes to the Bridge of Sighs in Venice, Antonio Contino's bridge over the Rio di Palazzo which was erected in the year 1600 to connect the Doge's prisons, or *Prigioni*, with the inquisitor's rooms in the main palace – the sighs being those of the condemned prisoners. In fact, Cambridge's Bridge of Sighs bears little resemblance to its Venetian namesake beyond the fact that both are covered bridges.

Despite its decorative appearance, commercial barges – towed by horses wading through the water on a gravelled causeway – still passed regularly under the bridge for many years after it was built, on their way to the mills at the upstream end of the town.

Bridge of Sighs, St John's College.

Wills's Cigarettes.

Arms of St John's College, Cambridge University.

ARMS OF OXFORD & CAMBRIDGE COLLEGES
A SERIES OF 42. No 17
WILLS'S CIGARETTES
ST. JOHN'S COLLEGE, CAMBRIDGE.
St. John's College, dedicated to the honour of St. John the Evangelist, was founded in 1511 by the Lady Margaret, Countess of Richmond and Derby, mother of Henry VII, and daughter and sole heir of John Beaufort, Duke of Somerset; and, like Christ's College, which she also founded, the College also bears the Arms of Beaufort, although in this case the Eagle of St. John is added as a crest, it being based upon an earlier foundation—that of the Hospital of St. John, founded about 1135. But the Countess died before all her plans had come to fruition, and the establishing of St. John's College was largely due to the energies and munificence of her executor John Fisher, Bishop of Rochester and Chancellor of the University.
W.D. & H.O. WILLS, Bristol & London.
ISSUED BY THE IMPERIAL TOBACCO COMPANY (OF GREAT BRITAIN & IRELAND), LIMITED.

PLATE 2

NORMAN CHURCH OF THE HOLY SEPULCHRE

The Round Church, in the heart of the Norman town, pre-dates the founding of the University by nearly a century.

In 1130, when the "Confraternity of the Holy Sepulchre" first built it, the Round Church must have been one of the most significant buildings in Cambridge. Its shape is thought to have been inspired by that of the Church of the Holy Sepulchre in Jerusalem, which the founders would have seen during the First Crusade. It stood at the junction of the two principal streets, not far from the Great Bridge – the commercial heart of the town – and was originally a chapel for travellers before becoming a parish church.

The building was modernised in the fifteenth century by the addition of a tall belfry, which stood for four centuries until part of the vaulted ceiling collapsed in the 1840s. At this point historians from the Camden Society were called in and advised a complete restoration of the church to its original Norman form.

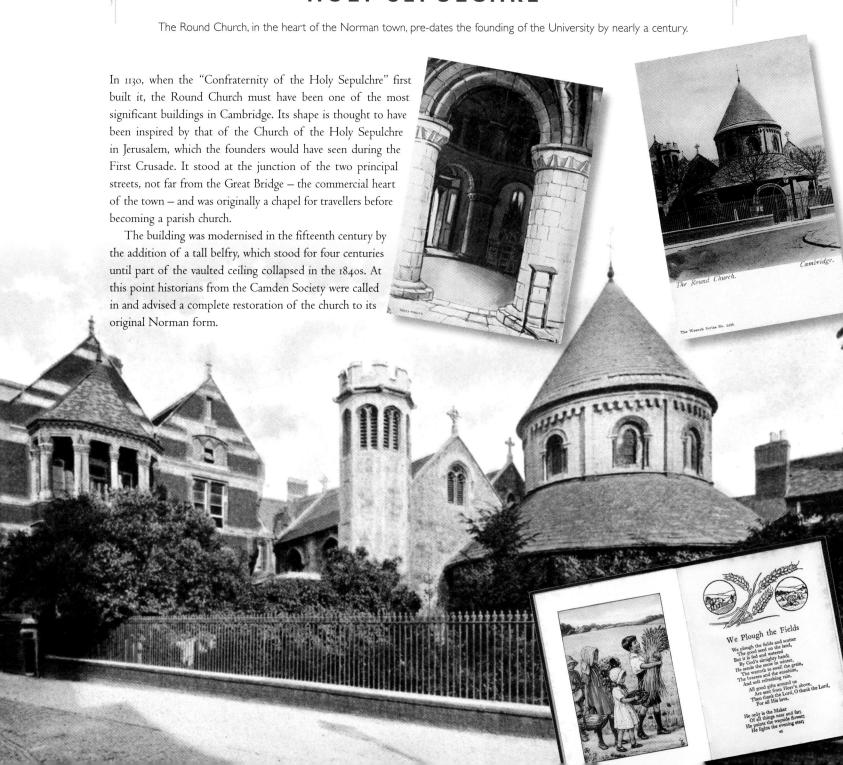

The Round Church.   Cambridge.

The Wrench Series No. 5296.

PLATE 3

MARKET SQUARE

Laid out in Victorian times, the market square is still the commercial and physical heart of the city.

Cambridge has had a market for many centuries, but its home in the present square in front of Great St Mary's Church (known as Market Hill, although it is completely flat) was only designed in the mid-nineteenth century. The opportunity arose because of a disastrous fire in September 1849 that destroyed many buildings on the site. Before that, the market was held in a smaller area to the south and east.

The ornate Victorian Gothic fountain was built in 1855 as a replacement for the head of Hobson's Conduit, which had stood in the marketplace supplying fresh water since 1614. The conduit head was reconstructed in Lensfield Road. The fountain has not proved to be so long-lived: in 1953 its superstructure was found to be unsafe and it was dismantled.

The wooden stalls used in Edwardian times could be taken down to clear the space between market days. The modern ones are permanent and are used every day.

PLATE 4

THE OLD GATEWAY OF KING'S COLLEGE

After centuries as the main entrance to King's College, the old gateway
in Trinity Lane now gives access to the University's offices.

When Henry VI founded King's College in 1441, he planned to locate the main buildings south of the chapel, and soon began buying up land for that purpose. However, the chosen site was not vacant: shops, houses, hostels, another college and a church would all have to go. Meanwhile, his builders started work on the chapel and a small court to the north of it, with a gateway onto Mill Street (now called Trinity Lane) opposite Clare College.

The Wars of the Roses disrupted Henry's plans, and he was deposed. For nearly three hundred years the main college site was just a garden, and the scholars made do with the cramped northern court.

Over time King's did acquire more buildings, and was finally able to dispense with the northern court. In 1828 the undergraduates moved out and the college sold the court to the University authorities, who had long occupied the site just behind it. The University demolished most of the original court but retained and expanded the gateway, which now serves as the entrance to its administrative offices in the Old Schools.

PLATE 5

ST JOHN'S COLLEGE GATEWAY
AND TOWER FROM TRINITY STREET

Sixteenth-century buildings belonging to Cambridge's two largest colleges stand side by side
along the street, with the Victorian Gothic chapel of St John's visible behind.

William Wordsworth would have passed frequently through the Tudor Great Gate to his room in St John's College. In 1806 he wrote in *The Prelude*:

> The Evangelist St. John my patron was:
> Three Gothic courts are his, and in the first
> Was my abiding-place, a nook obscure;
> Right underneath, the College kitchens made
> A humming sound ...

He was also very familiar with Trinity's Tudor chapel next door:

> And from my pillow, looking forth by light
> Of moon or favouring stars, I could behold
> The antechapel where the statue stood
> Of Newton ...

One of the elements in the present view from Trinity Street that would have surprised him is the chapel of St John's. He would have worshipped in a modest thirteenth-century building which the college had inherited from the old St John's Hospital. This, along with the whole north side of First Court, was swept away to make room for Sir George Gilbert Scott's grand Gothic Revival edifice, finished in 1869.

PLATE 6

ORIEL WINDOW OF THE HALL, TRINITY GREAT COURT

Great Court, by far the largest court in Cambridge, has enough space along its western side
for both the grand dining hall and the substantial Elizabethan lodge where the Master lives.

The hall of Trinity, with its hammer-beamed ceiling, minstrels' gallery and portrait of Henry VIII (a copy of the Holbein original) is the largest college dining hall in Cambridge. The master's lodge is also a remarkable building – its Tudor drawing room has a gold-embossed ceiling and an ornamented fireplace – but as a private residence it is much less familiar to visitors.

The Trinity Hall College

Two notable occupants of the lodge were Dr Henry Montagu Butler, whose thirty-year tenure as Master covered the period before and after 1900, and his young wife Agnata. As Agnata Frances Ramsay of Girton College she had astounded the University establishment in 1887 by attaining the highest marks in the Classical Tripos. She was not, of course, awarded a degree: another sixty years would pass before the first Cambridge degree was conferred on a woman. Dr Butler, who was 57 years old and a widower when he married the 21-year-old Miss Ramsay, had always supported the admission of women to the University.

PLATE 7

THE OLD CASTLE INN

As the twentieth century opened, Cambridge made an important concession to the modern world:
townswomen could now walk the streets without fear of imprisonment by the University authorities.

In the nineteenth century the University's Proctors, often seen patrolling the streets, were responsible for disciplining undergraduates, fining them for not wearing their gowns or confining them to their colleges for more serious offences. But it was their powers over people who were not members of the University that struck outsiders as remarkable. Charters from the sixteenth century meant that they could lawfully arrest anyone they thought to be of undesirable character. Suspects were tried in a special court, in private, by the Vice-Chancellor. By the nineteenth century those convicted were mainly local women, caught in the company of undergraduates and accused of prostitution; they could be sentenced to confinement for several days in the notorious Spinning House.

All this changed in 1894 when a young woman called Daisy Hopkins dragged the University through the public courts and shamed it into voluntarily giving up its right of imprisonment. The Spinning House was pulled down, and in 1901 the solemn grey bulk of a modern police station, visible just beyond the cheerful window-boxes of the Castle Inn, appeared in its place.

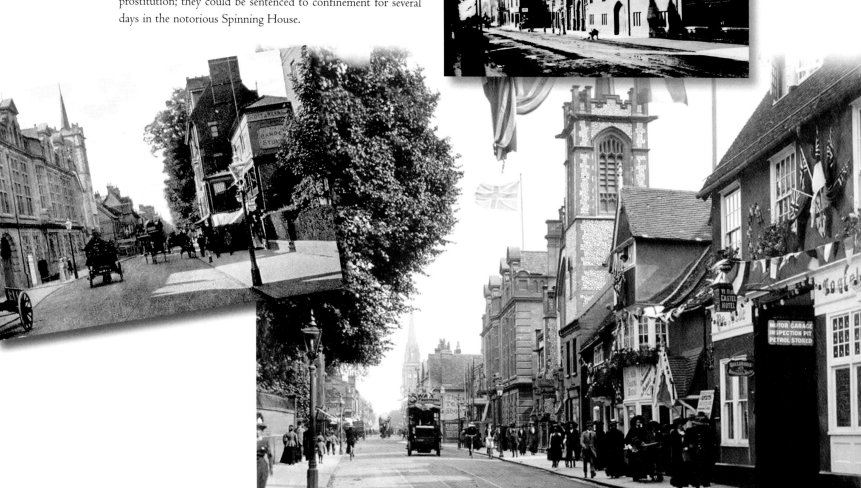

PLATE 8

PETERHOUSE FROM THE STREET

Four buildings in strongly contrasting architectural styles form an interesting composition
along Trumpington Street – arranged in chronological order as if intended to illustrate a history lecture.

First in the street, and earliest, is Peterhouse's Perne Library with its oriel window, dating from 1633. It is followed by the very unusual Baroque east front of Peterhouse chapel, which was completed in 1665. After that is Sir James Burrough's building of 1736, also part of Peterhouse, with its smart Ketton stone facings – part of a symmetrical neo-Palladian design, never completed, that was to replace the college's first court. Finally, to the right of the picture is the spire of the Emmanuel Congregational church, which became a United Reformed church later in the twentieth century. This was designed in 1873 by Joseph Cubitt, and demonstrates the Victorians' love affair with the medieval world: its style is copied from that common in France in the thirteenth century.

A herd of sheep being driven up the street in the direction of the Market Square would not have been an uncommon sight in Edwardian times, as meat for the table often arrived in town on the hoof.

PLATE 9

PETERHOUSE – THE FIRST COURT

The first court of Peterhouse, which is both the oldest and the smallest college in Cambridge,
is dominated by its unusual seventeenth-century chapel.

In 1284 Hugo de Balsham, the Bishop of Ely, purchased two houses in Trumpington Street and founded a new establishment to accommodate fourteen "worthy but impoverished Fellows". There were already scholars in Cambridge, and indeed they had already formed themselves into a University (a copy of their original Statutes from about 1250 still survives), but this was the first step in the development of the collegiate system.

The chapel of Peterhouse, joined to the buildings on either side of it by cloisters, was built during the seventeenth century when the Master of the college was Matthew Wren, uncle to Sir Christopher Wren. Its style mixes Renaissance details with a traditional Gothic design, and its unusually shaped skyline resembles nothing else in English architecture. The chapel was much admired in the nineteenth century when the Gothic style was beginning to find favour again: Pugin wrote that it was an example of a building where "many of the old principles were retained".

Wills's Cigarettes.

Arms of Peterhouse or St Peter's College. Cambridge University.

Front Court, St. Peter's College, Cambridge

ARMS OF OXFORD & CAMBRIDGE COLLEGES
A SERIES OF 42. No 12
WILLS'S CIGARETTES
PETERHOUSE, CAMBRIDGE.

Peterhouse, or (to give the place its full name) St. Peter's College, is the oldest College in the University of Cambridge, having been founded in 1284 by Hugh of Balsham, Bishop of Ely, for a Master and fourteen Fellows. The present statutes governing the foundation date from 1882. There are twenty-one open Scholarships, four of these being of the value of £80 per annum, and ten of the value of £60. The Master of the College is elected by the Fellows, and the Fellows from the Graduates of the College, or other Graduates of Oxford or Cambridge. The Arms, which were granted by Robert Cooke, Clarenceux King of Arms, in 1572, are supposed to be based upon the Arms of the founder, the bordure around the shield carrying a repetition of the open crowns from the Arms of the Bishopric of Ely.

W.D.& H.O.WILLS, Bristol & London
ISSUED BY THE IMPERIAL TOBACCO COMPANY
(OF GREAT BRITAIN & IRELAND), LIMITED.

PLATE 10

PETERHOUSE FROM THE FELLOWS' GARDEN

A range of very ancient buildings, with views of the college's garden and deer park,
forms the southern side of Peterhouse's Old Court.

The thirteenth-century dining hall of Peterhouse is the oldest purpose-built college building in Cambridge; there are older structures in Jesus College, but they were inherited from the convent that used to stand on the same site. The Combination Room (the Fellows' Parlour) was added at the eastern end in 1460; both it and the dining hall overlook the Fellows' Garden.

There was a long period when medieval architecture was not much admired, and as a result Peterhouse's old buildings were modernised during the eighteenth century. With the revival of interest in the Gothic during Queen Victoria's reign, the college undertook a programme of "re-Gothicisation": George Gilbert Scott worked on the architecture and the Pre-Raphaelites William Morris, Ford Madox Brown and Edward Burne-Jones contributed some excellent stained glass.

Beyond the garden there is a more open area of the grounds, which forms the smallest deer park in England. The college really did use it for keeping a herd of deer, introduced during the nineteenth century, until after the First World War.

PLATE 11

CLARE COLLEGE AND BRIDGE
FROM THE CAM – AUTUMN EVENING

For several centuries Clare College had just one building, an extraordinarily handsome
four-storey square court, with its own beautiful bridge over the river.

As this college had remained quite small – in 1870 it still had only seventy undergraduates – the original court was sufficient for its needs, and it did not build anything more until the 1920s.

Clare Bridge, which was built in the classical style, dates from 1640. Its parapet is decorated with fourteen large stone balls, from one of which a segment of the stone is mysteriously absent. This missing slice has given rise to many fanciful stories, the most enduring of which – though it is probably not true – being that the original builder removed it because his bill had not been paid in full.

The bridge is the oldest still surviving in Cambridge. Several older bridges were destroyed during the Civil War by the parliamentarian troops who had control of the town and most of the colleges, in order to make it easier to defend against an attack from the west.

CLARE COLLEGE AND BRIDGE FROM THE AVENUE

The walk from the centre of Cambridge through Clare College
and over its bridge to the Backs has always been a delightful one.

Just before the Civil War, Clare Hall (as the college was then
called) began a 77-year project to demolish its existing buildings
and construct a new and still much-admired court on the same
site. It had just acquired the area of land known as Butt Close, on
the opposite bank of the river, where it later created the Fellows'
Garden. The beautiful wrought iron gates that give access from
Clare Bridge to Butt Close, decorated with cut-sheet acanthus and
laurel foliage, were made in 1714.

Everyone in the Edwardian upper and middle classes – man,
woman and child – wore a hat, and for a fashionable lady the
hat was usually a dramatic affair, with an elegantly curving brim
sweeping around the face. The illusion that the hat was suspended
by magic above the lady's head was fostered by the careful use of
hair supports, on which a voluminous puffed-up hairstyle was
built. The hat could then be pinned to the hair.

Clare College from the Bridge, Cambridge

HARRY. MORLEY

E. W. HASLEHURST.

PLATE 13

THE HALL OF CLARE COLLEGE

Clare, a small but very beautiful college, has produced its share of distinguished graduates,
including one who became a famous martyr.

Clare College was founded in a very small way in 1326; a few years later its name was changed to Clare Hall when it was given a more generous endowment by a new benefactor, Lady Elizabeth de Clare, a member of the royal family. She intended her college to promote "the knowledge of letters … when it hath been found, it sendeth forth its students, who have tasted of its sweetness, fit and proper members in God's Church and the State, to rise to diverse heights, according to the claim of

their deserts". A bust of Lady Elizabeth appears over the chimney-piece in the Hall.

Notable among Clare's graduates is Hugh Latimer, whose portrait also hangs in the Hall. He became chaplain to King Henry VIII during the latter's marriage to Anne Boleyn, and supported the king's decision to dissolve the monasteries. Latimer refused to turn back into a Catholic twenty years later when Queen Mary's accession made it advisable, and was burned at the stake for his decision.

PLATE 14

THE OLD COURT, PEMBROKE COLLEGE

A generation earlier, a lady seen in college escorted by a don could only have been a visitor; by Edwardian times, however, she could well have been his wife.

The 1880s saw a revolution in the domestic life of Cambridge University. The heads of colleges and some professors had long been permitted to have wives, but a survival of the monastic tradition had dictated that the Fellows must be single. For many men this had meant that a college fellowship was not a life-long career: on marriage they left Cambridge, often becoming clergymen. This all changed with the late nineteenth-century reforms, and the change had a profound effect on the structure of the town as streets of late-Victorian and Edwardian middle-class houses sprang up to accommodate the academics' families.

Pembroke's late-Victorian dining hall, shown on the right of this painting, was designed by Alfred Waterhouse, and replaced a fourteenth-century original. Waterhouse's building was to be modernised in its turn during the 1920s, with the Gothic tracery removed from the windows and two new storeys of rooms added above.

PLATE 15

A COURT AND CLOISTERS
IN PEMBROKE COLLEGE

Pembroke College's Baroque chapel, beyond the cloisters, is the first building
designed by Sir Christopher Wren, the architect of St Paul's Cathedral.

Matthew Wren, who had been a Fellow of Pembroke
and chaplain to King Charles I, was imprisoned by
Oliver Cromwell. He vowed to donate a large sum of
money for "some holy and pious employment" on his
release, which eventually came eighteen years later when
the monarchy had been restored. He decided to fulfil his
promise by giving a grand new chapel to his old college,
and he employed his nephew, Christopher Wren, as the
architect. The design is notable because this was the first
entirely Classical chapel to be built in Cambridge, and it
represented a radical change from the many centuries of
building in the Gothic style that had preceded it.

Gardens have always been an important part of the
college environment, and Pembroke's are particularly fine.
Such beauty is not maintained without a lot of hard work:
many generations of Cambridge
people have found employment
with the colleges as gardeners.

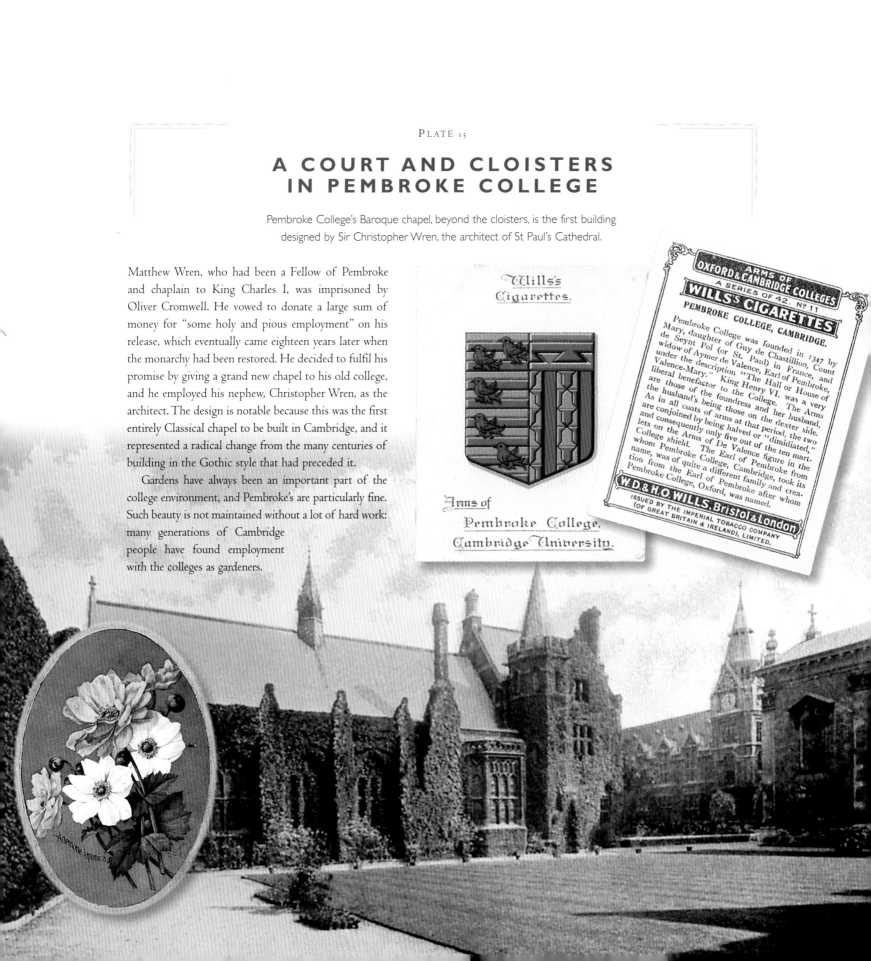

Wills's
Cigarettes.

Arms of
Pembroke College,
Cambridge University.

ARMS OF
OXFORD & CAMBRIDGE COLLEGES
A SERIES OF 42. Nº 11
WILLS'S CIGARETTES
PEMBROKE COLLEGE, CAMBRIDGE.

Pembroke College was founded in 1347 by
Mary, daughter of Guy de Chastillion, Count
de Seynt Pol (or St, Paul) in France, and
widow of Aymer de Valence, Earl of Pembroke,
under the description "The Hall or House of
Valence-Mary." King Henry VI. was a very
liberal benefactor to the College. The Arms
are those of the foundress and her husband,
the husband's being those on the dexter side.
As in all coats of arms at that period, the two
are conjoined by being halved or "dimidiated,"
and consequently only five out of the ten mart-
lets on the Arms of De Valence figure in the
College shield. The Earl of Pembroke from
whom Pembroke College, Cambridge, took its
name, was of quite a different family and crea-
tion from the Earl of Pembroke after whom
Pembroke College, Oxford, was named.

W.D.&H.O. WILLS. Bristol & London
ISSUED BY THE IMPERIAL TOBACCO COMPANY
(OF GREAT BRITAIN & IRELAND), LIMITED.

Anemone japonica

PLATE 16

TRINITY HALL

The main buildings of Trinity Hall, squeezed into a small riverside site
between Clare and Trinity, are not imposing, but they are very charming.

After half of England's population had been wiped out by the
Black Death of 1349, there was a national shortage of both
clergymen and lawyers. Bishop William Bateman of Norwich,
a diocese which had lost nearly 700 priests, founded a new
Cambridge college in 1350 "for the promotion of divine worship
and of canon and civil science and direction of the commonwealth
and especially of our church and diocese of Norwich". Although
it has never been a large college, it has remained particularly
strong in the study of legal matters ever since.

Trinity Hall would probably have changed its name to Trinity
College – other early foundations changed theirs from Hall to
College – but Henry VIII had already used the name, so Trinity
Hall it remained.

The college buildings are surrounded by delightful gardens.
Henry James said: "If I were called upon to mention the prettiest
corner of the world, I should draw a thoughtful sigh and point
the way to the gardens of Trinity Hall."

The Chapel
Trinity Hall

PLATE 17

ST BOTOLPH'S CHURCH AND CORPUS COLLEGE FROM THE STEPS OF THE PITT PRESS, TRUMPINGTON STREET

King's Parade – known in earlier centuries as the High Street – has always been the place where the dual nature of Cambridge is most obvious to visitors.

Right in front of Corpus, King's and St Catharine's Colleges, and the ancient St Botolph's and Great St Mary's churches, the ordinary life of the town carries on.

Tram lines were put in along Trumpington Street and King's Parade in 1880 and the horse-drawn tram service was an immediate success, despite initial opposition from some conservative dons (one Professor Newton made his disapproval felt by walking slowly between the lines in front of Great St Mary's). The route ran from Hyde Park Corner, where it met another line coming from the railway station, to the terminus at the market place. Although some passengers worried about the trams overturning when taking the sharp corner in front of the Senate House, there is no record of them having done so.

Motor omnibuses were introduced during the Edwardian era, and by the First World War they had superseded the trams. The lines were taken up in the 1920s.

PLATE 18

THE OLD COURT,
CORPUS CHRISTI COLLEGE

Corpus Christi's Old Court, dating from the 1350s, is in fact the oldest court
anywhere in Cambridge; it probably also predates the oldest one in Oxford.

Corpus Christi is unique: it is the only college in either Oxford or Cambridge to have been founded by townspeople, and it still celebrates this fact by inviting councillors and other prominent local people to an annual feast.

The founders were the wealthy guilds of Corpus Christi and St Mary in the parish of St Bene't's (shortened from Benedict's). They received their licence to found a college from King Edward III in 1352, and immediately began to construct the first modest court right next to their own parish church. Old Court still retains many fascinating early architectural features, such as the sills and jambs that held pieces of oil-soaked linen to cover the windows before the days of glass window-panes.

Wills's
Cigarettes.

Arms of
Corpus Christi College,
Cambridge University.

ARMS OF
OXFORD & CAMBRIDGE COLLEGES
A SERIES OF 42. No 4
WILLS'S CIGARETTES

CORPUS CHRISTI COLLEGE,
CAMBRIDGE.

Corpus Christi College, Cambridge, was founded in 1352 by two Trade Guilds at that time in existence in Cambridge. These were the Guild of Corpus Christi and the Guild of the Blessed Virgin Mary, and these Guilds having united into one about the year 1350, with the name of "The Guild of the Body of Jesus Christ and His Mother the Virgin Mary," obtained with the assistance of Henry, Duke of Lancaster, whose aid was invoked, and who was an Alderman of the Consolidated Guild, a license dated Nov. 7, 1352, from King Edward III. for founding a College, to be called "The Home of the Scholars of Corpus Christi and the Blessed Virgin Mary." The Arms were granted in 1570 by Cooke, Clarenceux King of Arms, at the cost of Archbishop Parker.

W. D. & H. O. WILLS, Bristol & London

ISSUED BY THE IMPERIAL TOBACCO COMPANY
(OF GREAT BRITAIN & IRELAND), LIMITED.

PLATE 19

ST BENEDICT'S CHURCH
FROM FREE SCHOOL LANE

An early twentieth-century visitor to Free School Lane would have been able
to marvel at a striking juxtaposition of the very old and the very new.

Anglo-Saxon Cambridge seems to have been arranged in two separate settlements, one based on the old Roman town near the Great Bridge, and the other a short walk to the south of it, centred around what is now Bene't Street. St Benedict's (St Bene't's) Church is the oldest surviving building in the city, and its tower, which predates the Norman Conquest, is the oldest part of it.

The wall beside this ancient chapel belongs to Corpus Christi, and is the oldest surviving fragment of college architecture. On the opposite side of the lane is the original home of the

Cavendish Laboratory, where J.J. Thompson discovered the electron in 1897. A few years later, under the directorship of Ernest Rutherford, researchers at the Cavendish were the first to split the atom.

The "Free School" itself dates from the seventeenth century, when Dr Stephen Perse left money in his will for the education of a hundred local boys.

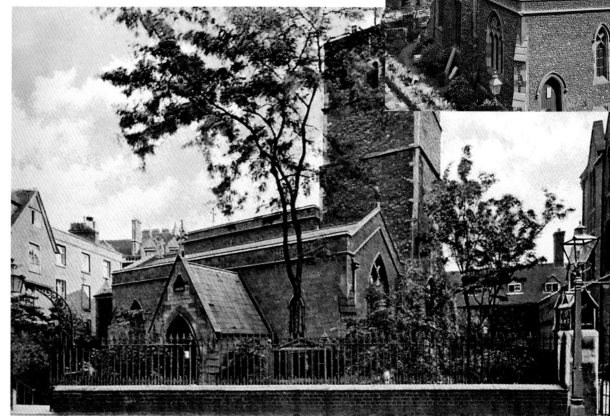

PLATE 20

KING'S COLLEGE GATEWAY AND CHAPEL – TWILIGHT EFFECT

Many people assume that the screen and gateway that form the street frontage of King's College are as old as the chapel, but in fact they date only from the 1820s.

For several centuries King's was just a magnificent chapel with a very small college attached. This had begun to change by the eighteenth century, when the Gibbs Building was completed, and by the 1820s sufficient funds had been raised to pay for the next stage of the project. The college held a competition to select an architect and the winner was William Wilkins, who went on to design the screen, the gateway and the college dining hall.

The tall railings that divided the college from King's Parade in Edwardian times formed an "iron curtain" behind which undergraduates could saunter, separate from the bustle of the street outside with its hackney cabs and trams. In 1927 this barrier between "town" and "gown" was removed when the railings were taken down to improve the view. They were replaced by a low stone wall.

Wills's
Cigarettes.

Arms of
King's College,
Cambridge University

ARMS OF
OXFORD & CAMBRIDGE COLLEGES
A SERIES OF 42. Nº 9
WILLS'S CIGARETTES
KING'S COLLEGE, CAMBRIDGE.

King's College, Cambridge, was founded and endowed in 1441 by King Henry VI., for a Provost and seventy Scholars, each vacancy to be filled up by the admission of a Scholar from the sister establishment at Eton, which the King founded concurrently. The connection between the two establishments is still maintained by the fact that of the forty-eight Foundation Scholarships which exist, one half are exclusively appropriated to scholars from Eton. The Arms of this College were granted directly by King Henry VI. himself by Letters Patent, dated Jan. 1, 1449, as were the Arms of Eton.

W. D. & H. O. WILLS, Bristol & London
ISSUED BY THE IMPERIAL TOBACCO COMPANY
(OF GREAT BRITAIN & IRELAND), LIMITED.

PLATE 21

GATEWAY OF KING'S COLLEGE, KING'S PARADE

King's Parade is a shopping street as well as being the heart of the University;
until the nineteenth century there were shops along both sides of it.

Most of the shops on the western side of the street were cleared away during the nineteenth century to make room for new buildings for King's College. Further down, where the name of the road changes to Trumpington Street, a row of shops was demolished to make way for the expansion of St Catharine's College.

By the early twentieth century several tailors, outfitters and robemakers were carrying on their businesses on the eastern side of King's Parade, opposite King's College. There were also shops here selling prints and framing pictures, as well as bookshops, a tobacconist's, a restaurant and a chemist's shop. The chemist was called Deck, and he was responsible for firing the rocket every New Year's Eve outside the gates of King's College, a long-standing custom that was stopped by the First World War but restarted in 1919, moving to Parker's Piece. Visitors would have been amused to note that three of King's Parade's shopkeepers bore the names Sadd, Greef and Pain.

Opposite King's Chapel.

J. G. BUOL,
Swiss Cafe and Restaurant,
17, KING'S PARADE, CAMBRIDGE.

EXCELLENT TEA, COFFEE, CHOCOLATE
Freshly made for Each Customer.
High Class Dining, Coffee, Smoking and Private Rooms.
Breakfasts, Luncheons or Dinner a la Carte at any time.
Table d'Hote from 6 to 9 p.m.
Luncheon or Tea Baskets supplied on the Shortest Notice.
ESTIMATES GIVEN.
Caterers for Balls, Garden Parties, Weddings, Etc.

PLATE 22

KING'S COLLEGE CHAPEL AND THE ENTRANCE COURT, FROM THE FELLOWS' BUILDINGS

Central to King Henry VI's vision for King's College was the choir, and in particular
its regular commitment to singing at services in the Chapel.

The Statutes of King's provide for the maintenance of sixteen choristers, who were to be "poor and needy boys, of sound condition and honest conversation, being ascertainable under the age of twelve years, knowing how to read and sing". They were to "assist daily the priest celebrating in the chapel, and also in the hall to assist the other servants of the King's College by humbly and honestly ministering and serving the said fellows at table".

Provision for educating the choristers developed over the centuries, and by Edwardian times a boarding school had been established for them in West Road. A few non-singing boys also attended, and by 1911 it had forty pupils. The choirboys would – as they still do – march across the Backs in procession to sing at services in the Chapel.

In the early twentieth century the college introduced choral scholarships, which provided an income for fourteen undergraduates who would also serve as members of the choir.

PLATE 23

KING'S COLLEGE CHAPEL AND THE FELLOWS' BUILDINGS

The two most striking buildings of King's College must have presented a startling contrast when they were first seen side by side.

King's College Chapel is the culmination of the Gothic style of architecture, the style of the Middle Ages. This had been gradually refined over a period of several centuries, during which archways had grown more and more delicate and pinnacles ever more breathtakingly ornate.

After the burst of activity that finally completed the chapel, almost two centuries were to pass before King's College was ready to start on another major building project. At that time the idea of designing anything new along the same lines would have been quite unthinkable. The neo-classical Gibbs Building, named after the architect who designed it in 1724, must have represented a solid step forward into the modern world. Fortunately Gibbs was an admirer of the Gothic chapel, and he took care to place his new building in a pleasing relationship to it, leaving enough empty space between the two so that the extreme contrast in styles would not offend the eye.

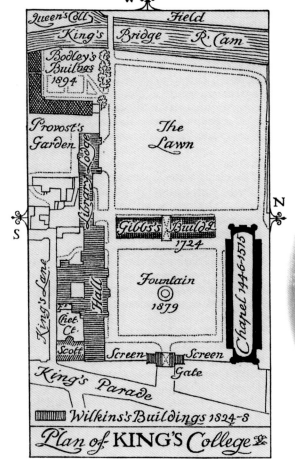

Plan of KING'S College

Chapel & Gibbs's Buildings.

KING'S COLLEGE CHAPEL
INTERIOR FROM THE CHOIR

The long delays that the Wars of the Roses caused in the construction
of King's College Chapel proved to be a blessing in disguise.

When Henry VI lost his throne the funds for his project to build a college and a vast chapel in Cambridge dried up, and the building stood partly completed for several decades. Meanwhile, master stonemasons were working elsewhere to perfect the design of ever more elaborate vaulted stone ceilings, with ever more delicate carving. When, eventually, a chest full of money arrived from Henry VII to pay for the work here to be continued, a truly exquisite fan vault – the world's largest – was constructed in a period of just three years.

The chapel was finally completed during the reign of Henry VIII, who paid for most of the interior woodwork, the carving of which includes a liberal scattering of Tudor roses. The magnificent stained-glass windows also date from this period – all except for the huge west window, which is Victorian.

The chapel as a whole represents the ultimate refinement of the Gothic style of architecture after centuries of development.

PLATE 25

THE HALL OF KING'S COLLEGE

The revolutionary changes that took place within Cambridge University
during the second half of the nineteenth century were nowhere more evident than at King's College.

Augustus Austen-Leigh, one of Jane Austen's great-nephews, was Provost of King's from 1889 until his death in 1905. Under his leadership the academic life of the College was transformed as thoroughly as its buildings had been seventy years before. The College had begun as an exclusive, luxurious club for old Etonians – it had been associated with Eton by Henry VI, who founded both, and it was closed to pupils of other schools until the 1860s, but within a single generation it had developed into one of the most dynamic, liberal and forward-looking colleges in Cambridge, nurturing such towering twentieth-century intellects as E.M. Forster, who studied there until 1901, and John Maynard Keynes, who gained his BA in 1905 and subsequently became a lecturer.

The dining hall at King's, although it looks much older, is part of the Tudor-Gothic-style development that was designed for the college by William Wilkins in the 1820s.

PLATE 26

ENTRANCE GATEWAY, QUEENS' COLLEGE

The medieval Queens' College was the prototype for a new kind
of building that was to be repeated all over the city.

Founded in 1448 by Margaret of Anjou, the wife of Henry VI, Queens' College was refounded in the following reign by Elizabeth Woodville, the wife of Edward IV. As there are two Queens involved, not one, getting the apostrophe in the right place in this college's name is one of the small pieces of gleeful pedantry by which generations of Cambridge insiders have recognised one another.

Front Court at Queens', with its gatehouse in Queens' Lane, is the earliest fully developed Cambridge college court, a style of building that was later imitated many times, and is one of the best-preserved examples of medieval college architecture in the city. The eastern range, which includes the gatehouse, was the first part to be constructed; its brickwork is only a facing, being filled in behind with rubble. The huge oak gates with their wrought iron hinges are the original ones from 1448.

Wills's
Cigarettes.

Arms of
Queen's College.
Cambridge University.

Queen's College, Cambridge

Valentines Series

ARMS OF
OXFORD & CAMBRIDGE COLLEGES
A SERIES OF 42. № 13
WILLS'S CIGARETTES
QUEENS' COLLEGE, CAMBRIDGE.

This College has two Queens for its founders—namely, Margaret of Anjou, the wife of King Henry VI., who founded it in 1448, and Elizabeth Widville, wife of King Edward IV., who refounded it in 1465. This College has used a variety of different shields, but it is perhaps typical of the unpopularity of King Edward IV.'s Queen, that when in 1575, Cooke, Clarenceux, granted Arms to the College, these should have been those of Queen Margaret of Anjou, without any reference to the later Queen. The College, however, preserves her memory by placing the possessive comma after the "s" instead of before it.

W. D. & H. O. WILLS, Bristol & London
IMPERIAL TOBACCO COMPANY
(IN & IRELAND), LIMITED.

PLATE 27

AN OLD COURT IN QUEENS' COLLEGE

The Long Gallery, which serves as part of the President's Lodge, is an Elizabethan
half-timbered building, but its timbers were hidden behind plaster until 1911.

Shortly after this painting was completed, Queens' College made radical changes to the buildings depicted in it. Within four years the battlements that had decorated the Hall since the 1860s were taken down; the plaster that had covered the half-timbered front of the Long Gallery was removed; and the Victorian clock tower, visible over the roof of the Hall, disappeared.

Most colleges are headed by Masters, but Queens' has a President. Dr Humphry Tyndall, the President who was responsible for the construction of the beautifully panelled Long Gallery, seems to have had a very keen awareness of his own generosity: his will (he died in 1614) says "I give to the president and fellows of Queens college in Cambridge to my successors use of all the seeling [ceiling] and wainscoting of my chambers and lodging I have, which I take amounteth to two hundred and fifty pounds or thereabouts more than I have received from the college or any other benefactors towards the same".

PLATE 28

QUEENS' COLLEGE
FROM THE RIVER FRONT

The Mathematical Bridge, the charming wooden footbridge at Queens' College,
is the subject of one of Cambridge's most enduring myths.

The story goes that the original designer of the Mathematical Bridge (Isaac Newton himself, in some versions of the tale) was so skilled in mechanics that he constructed it without using any bolts or screws, the wooden planks being placed at precise angles so as to stay in position unaided. Lesser scholars, not content simply to admire the master's handiwork, took it apart to find out how it worked, were unable to repeat the trick, and had to resort to traditional methods when reconstructing it. This story is completely untrue: in fact the original builders of the bridge in 1749 used bolts from the beginning. It has been reconstructed twice but to essentially the same design.

In the distance beyond the Mathematical Bridge, two large watermills can be seen in Matthison's painting. These are the King's and Bishop's Mills, which were still in use for grinding corn in 1907. They were not pulled down until 1928.

PLATE 29

GATEWAY OF
ST CATHARINE'S COLLEGE

In the seventeenth century, Catharine Hall demolished most of its buildings and constructed
a new range – shown in the painting – along Milne Street (Queens' Lane) opposite Queens' College.

Work on Catharine Hall's new buildings (Mildred Tuker misspelled it "Catherine" in her book, as many people do) was much hampered by a long-running dispute with Queens' College, which owned land immediately to the south. In 1676 Catharine Hall's accounts include a payment "for pulling down five weeks' work" and, a little later, one for "pulling down next Queens'". The results of these adjustments can still be seen in the odd arrangement of windows where the building joins the southern range.

The Hall (renamed St Catharine's College in Victorian times) had been founded in the fifteenth century by Robert Wodelarke, then Provost of King's, who had fewer resources than most other college founders: at the beginning there were only funds to support three Fellows and a Master, whose duties were to study philosophy and theology and to conduct requiem masses for Wodelarke's soul.

The college's modern front entrance on Trumpington Street did not come into existence until much later when the land for it, then occupied by houses, was bequeathed to the college. Today the college uses its ancient coat of arms, which shows a catharine wheel in honour of St Catharine.

Wills's
Cigarettes.

Arms of
St Catharine's College.
Cambridge University.

ARMS OF
OXFORD & CAMBRIDGE COLLEGES
A SERIES OF 42. No 16
WILLS'S CIGARETTES
ST. CATHARINE'S COLLEGE,
CAMBRIDGE.

St. Catharine's College was founded in 1473 by Dr. Robert Woodlarke, Chancellor of the University of Cambridge, for a Master and three Fellows, and he was the first Master of the College. It has since been considerably augmented by different benefactions—notably that of Mrs. Mary Ramsden, of Norton and Fockerby, in County York. Of the twenty-six Scholarships, fourteen, each of the annual value of £40, were founded by Mrs. Ramsden. As no Arms have ever been granted to this College, different versions have been in use, but a note in the Visitation of 1684 states that the more simple one of a plain Katherine-wheel (the device of St. Katharine) was anciently used.

W.D.& H.O.WILLS, Bristol & London
ISSUED BY THE IMPERIAL TOBACCO COMPANY
(OF GREAT BRITAIN & IRELAND), LIMITED.

PLATE 30

GATEWAY OF JESUS COLLEGE

When Jesus College was founded, at the end of the Middle Ages, it was described
as being "near" Cambridge rather than "in" the town, and it still gives an unusually spacious, open impression.

The entrance to Jesus is unique: the gatehouse is approached via a walled pathway called the "chimney". The arrangement of the buildings inside is also unusual, being based on the existing buildings of a convent; every court, apart from the cloister, is open along at least one side.

The founder was John Alcock, who had been educated at Cambridge and in 1496 was Bishop of Ely as well as being a prominent statesman (he became Lord Chancellor twice and also served as an ambassador). He took over the buildings and grounds of the former Benedictine convent of St Radegund just outside the crowded medieval university town, and used them as the basis for "The College of the Blessed Virgin Mary, Saint John the Evangelist and the glorious Virgin Saint Radegund, near Cambridge"; it subsequently acquired the name of the chapel that had originally served the old nunnery. The Jesus Chapel had already stood for well over four centuries, and is the oldest building in any of the Cambridge colleges still in use today.

ARMS OF
OXFORD & CAMBRIDGE COLLEGES
A SERIES OF 42. No 8
WILL'S's CIGARETTES

JESUS COLLEGE, CAMBRIDGE.

Jesus College was founded in 1496 by John Alcock, Bishop of Ely and Chancellor of England, and now consists of a Master, sixteen Fellows, and at least twenty Scholars. One of the Scholarships attached to this College was founded by Richard Sterne, Archbishop of York, between 1664 and 1683, who was at one time Master of the College. The Arms were granted in 1575 by Robert Cooke, Clarenceux King of Arms, being the Arms of Alcock within a bordure of Ely, this being the same bordure which Cooke placed round the Arms of Peterhouse, which had at a much earlier date been founded by an earlier Bishop of Ely. There is no authority for the Bishop's mitre which is often placed in the centre of the fesse.

W.D. & H.O. WILLS. Bristol & London
ISSUED BY THE IMPERIAL TOBACCO COMPANY
(OF GREAT BRITAIN & IRELAND), LIMITED.

Wills's
Cigarettes.

Arms of
Jesus College,
Cambridge University.

Gateway, Jesus College, Cambridge

PLATE 31

THE GATEWAY OF CHRIST'S COLLEGE FROM ST ANDREW'S STREET

The buildings in this view of St Andrew's Street have changed very little since
it was painted, but the street scene has altered considerably.

The early-sixteenth-century gateway of Christ's appears slightly out of proportion as a result of a rise in the street level that has taken place since it was built, burying the base of the tower. The decorative coat of arms above the gate is that of Lady Margaret Beaufort, who founded the college in 1505 (and whose arms also appear on the gatehouse of St John's College, another of her foundations). Matthison chose his viewpoint carefully so as not to have to include the ornate tower of Foster's Bank.

A two-wheeled hansom cab waiting for a fare would have been a common sight in St Andrew's Street in Edwardian times, but it was not to remain so for long. As the distinguished scientist J.B.S. Haldane pointed out to a Cambridge audience in a 1923 lecture on *Science and the Future*, "now that romantic but tardy vehicle is a memory like the trireme, the velocipede, and the 1907 Voisin biplane".

Academics are no longer instantly recognisable in the street by their gowns and mortar-boards, though a long white beard and informal clothing might still provide a clue.

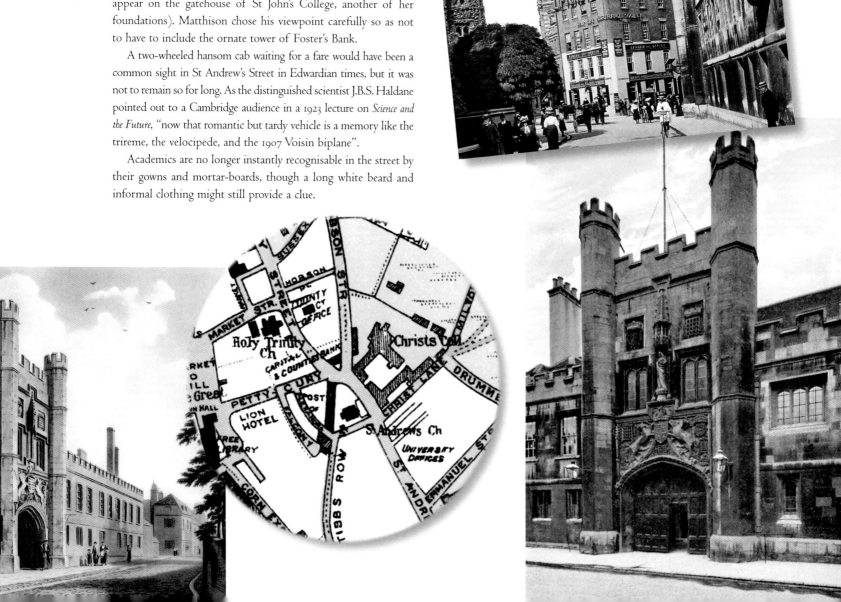

PLATE 32

THE FELLOWS' BUILDING IN CHRIST'S COLLEGE

Second Court in Christ's, open along one side, is the site of the handsome Fellows' Building – traditionally attributed, though without much evidence, to the great architect Inigo Jones.

After the Wars of the Roses, Lady Margaret Beaufort was one of the first people to realise that the future of learning lay with secular colleges rather than monasteries, and she set about founding schools and colleges; she also endowed professorships at both Oxford and Cambridge. Christ's was her first Cambridge college, and was created by re-founding an earlier institution called God's House that had been set up to train grammar-school masters.

During Elizabethan times Christ's became a leading Puritan college, and its adoption of this popular position resulted in a huge increase in student numbers in the early seventeenth century. The Fellows' Building, constructed during the 1640s after an appeal to the college's Fellows and alumni for funds, helped to ease the pressure on accommodation.

In the nineteenth century the college was notable for having educated Charles Darwin. It was the place where he first became interested in botany and geology, though his important work was all done after he had left Cambridge.

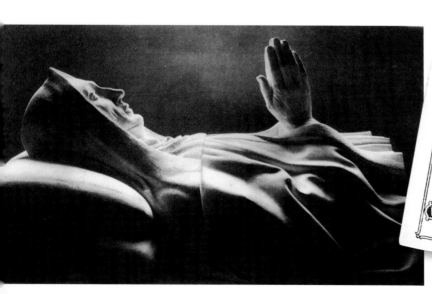

PLATE 33

MILTON'S MULBERRY TREE IN THE FELLOWS' GARDEN, CHRIST'S COLLEGE

The claim that it was John Milton himself who planted the mulberry in the garden of his college is probably false, but the tree is certainly old enough to have been known by him.

It is very likely that the mulberry tree generally known as "Milton's" was already established when he first arrived at the college in 1625. The first mulberry trees were planted here in 1608, the year the poet was born, and the two that remain – the

garden was laid out around them in 1825 – are probably survivors from that original planting. Both have suffered weather damage over the centuries and are now supported by earth piled up around the trunks, but they still produce fruit every year.

Milton spent seven years at Christ's, but his relationship with the college was rather strained. He said of his fellow students that "they thought themselves gallant men, and I thought them fools"; they in their turn termed him "the Lady of Christ's", and he was rusticated after a quarrel with his tutor. Perhaps he found solace in the pleasant shade of the mulberry tree, as many scholars have done since his time.

PLATE 34

THE GATEWAY AND TOWER OF ST JOHN'S COLLEGE

Where we now see a pleasant open space, a church stood for
nearly five hundred years until it was pulled down in 1865.

The unusual name of the former church, All Saints in the Jewry, comes from that of the Old Jewry district that lies between it and the Round Church. This had been the home of Cambridge's considerable Jewish population before its expulsion from the town in 1275 by the landowner Queen Eleanor, the widow of Henry III.

By 1865 the amount of traffic passing along the street had increased and the fifteenth-century church building, a replacement for the eleventh-century original, was deemed to be too much of an obstruction and

All Saints Church Cambridge

was pulled down. Jesus College, which had inherited the responsibility for this church along with the lands and buildings of the former St Radegund's nunnery, built a replacement for it in Jesus Lane, calling in William Morris to decorate the interior.

After the road had been widened the remaining part of the churchyard was turned into a garden.

PLATE 35

ENTRANCE TO ST JOHN'S COLLEGE CHAPEL FROM THE FIRST COURT

Originally constructed in 1511 when Lady Margaret Beaufort founded St John's,
First Court changed greatly as the college grew, and grew again.

This fine court, originally square, included all the elements a small college needed: a handsome gatehouse giving access from the street, a chapel – the thirteenth-century chapel of the former St John's Hospital – forming the northern side, and a dining hall next to it.

St John's, however, was not destined to stay small. Despite a setback during the Civil War when it found itself on the wrong side (the First Court was pressed into service as a prison by the victorious Parliamentary troops), it has expanded repeatedly, adding new courts in successive westward steps.

In the nineteenth century the college authorities decided to discard the pleasingly symmetrical layout of First Court so as to provide a hall and a chapel that were large enough for the hugely increased student population. The old chapel was demolished (its foundations are still visible in the grass) and replaced with a much larger one designed by Sir George Gilbert Scott; the hall was extended and given a huge new oriel window.

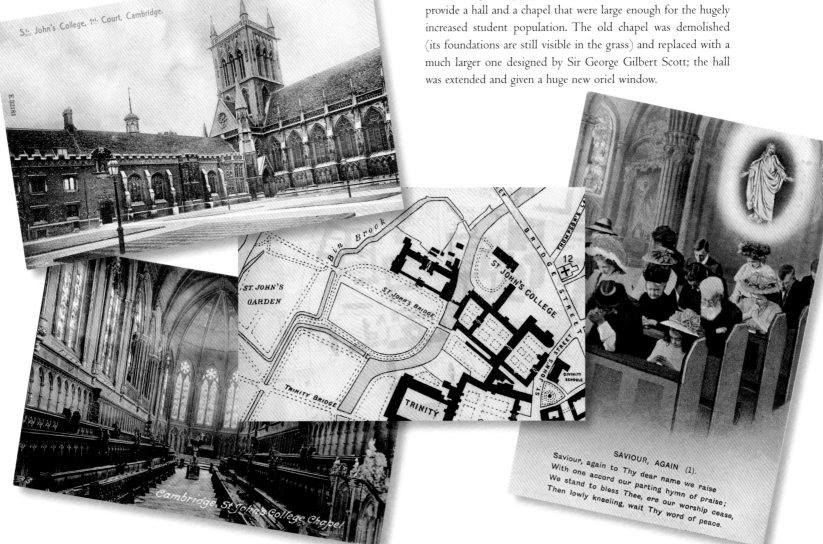

PLATE 36

THE SECOND COURT OF ST JOHN'S COLLEGE

St John's Second Court is Elizabethan, and was designed to form a harmonious whole.
Its fine brickwork is particularly admired.

The Tudor dining hall, shown to the right of the painting, has a particularly fine hammer-beam ceiling. It was cleverly extended in the nineteenth century.

The oriel window in the northern range of the court contains a stained-glass roundel that was made in about 1630 and shows a portrait of Queen Henrietta Maria. It commemorates the treaty between England and France that arranged her engagement to King Charles I. Tradition has it that this treaty was signed at St John's, in the room below the window.

In the centre of the western side of the court is a gatehouse called the Shrewsbury Tower. For a short while this formed the back entrance to the college until Third Court was added beyond it during the latter part of the seventeenth century. It is named after the Countess of Shrewsbury, who funded much of the building work in Second Court, and her statue and coat of arms appear on the front of it.

PLATE 37

THE COMBINATION ROOM, ST JOHN'S COLLEGE

In Cambridge the parlour of a college, where the Fellows meet to socialise after dinner, is called the "Combination Room". St John's College has a particularly fine example.

This first-floor gallery along the north range of the Elizabethan Second Court has panelled walls and a much-admired ornate plasterwork ceiling – the largest single unsupported ceiling in Cambridge. Modern additions such as electric lighting have never been allowed to intrude into the room, which is still lit by candles when it is used in the evening, just as it was when King Charles II dined here in 1681. It has been used by the Fellows as their Combination Room since 1864: before that time it was partitioned, and most of it formed part of what was then the Master's Lodge.

Several portraits of distinguished St John's graduates, and people who are important in the history of the college, hang in the Combination Room. These include the founder, Lady Margaret Beaufort (Henry VII's mother); the nineteenth-century mathematician and astronomer Sir John Herschel; and the social reformer William Wilberforce, who led the parliamentary campaign to abolish the slave trade.

"THE UNION" CIGAR STORES.
H. L. CASE,
Tobacconist,
65, BRIDGE STREET, CAMBRIDGE
(Opposite the Round Church).
Straight Cut Cigarettes a Speciality. All Goods of Finest Quality.
High Class Tobacco, Cigars, and Cigarettes.

PLATE 38

THE LIBRARY WINDOW, ST JOHN'S COLLEGE, FROM THE BRIDGE OF SIGHS

In the early twentieth century the old library of St John's College
was still in daily use by students and Fellows of the college.

John Williams, Bishop of Lincoln, donated the library to St John's College in 1624, and it is his Latin initials that appear over the bay window facing the Cam: the inscription reads "ILCS", which stands for "Iohannes Lincolniensis Custos Sigilli" (John of Lincoln, Lord Keeper of the Seal). The Bishop specified a very traditional style of architecture, which must have seemed old-fashioned to his contemporaries. Two centuries later, under the influence of the Gothic Revival, it would have elicited more admiration. The old library building now houses the college's special collections of rare books and manuscripts, and a modern working library has been constructed to the north of the chapel.

The Master's Lodge, a substantial house whose private walled garden leads down to the river beside the library, has its own entrance from Bridge Street. It was designed in the nineteenth century by Sir George Gilbert Scott, who was also the architect of the college chapel.

Oriel in library St John's College

PLATE 39

OLD GATEWAY AND BRIDGE

Late Victorian ladies and gentlemen took to the River Cam in rowing skiffs and canoes
with great enthusiasm – a boat trip was a popular way to admire the backs of the colleges.

Boats could be hired near Magdalene Bridge or, except on Sundays, from a raft moored behind Trinity College. Punts, which became so ubiquitous in Cambridge during the twentieth century, had only recently been introduced here from the Thames, and most people still preferred to row.

Boating for pleasure was still something relatively new. Just a few years earlier such close proximity to the water would have inspired a different emotion. As Gwen Raverat (born in 1885) wrote later: "I can remember the smell very well, for all the sewage went into the river, till the town was at last properly drained, when I was about ten years old. There is a tale of Queen Victoria being shown over Trinity by the Master, Dr Whewell, and saying, as she looked over the bridge: 'What are all those pieces of paper floating down the river?' To which, with great presence of mind, he replied: 'Those, ma'am, are notices that bathing is forbidden.'"

PAPER HANDKERCHIEFS

To be Destroyed after use.

That's what you do with a SILKY-FIBRE HANDKERCHIEF, which costs only 1/- for 50. This advantage is especially pleasant when you have Catarrh, or a cold, or during illness, when it is undesirable to use ordinary handkerchiefs twice and unpleasant to wash them. Then the name tells you how nice the material is, "SILKY-FIBRE" (Paper Chiffon).

50 for 1/-, 250, 4/3; at Chemists, or

"SILKY-FIBRE" DEPOT
3 UNITY ST., BRISTOL

Every Packet bears Registered Seal, "Toinoco Silky-Fibre."

PLATE 40

PEPYS' LIBRARY, MAGDALENE COLLEGE

Magdalene's attractive seventeenth-century library building houses the work of the college's most famous graduate.

Samuel Pepys is best remembered for the *Diary*, a vivid day-to-day account of both public and very private events that was not published until long after his death. He started writing it, in shorthand, when he was 27 years old and continued it for almost ten years.

In his later years, Pepys undertook another huge project: he decided to create a library of 3,000 volumes. He already had an impressive collection of books and prints, and now occupied his leisure hours in adding to it, employing a library clerk to help keep his books in order

and to add title pages, indexes and tables of contents. When he died in 1703 he had just reached his goal, and he bequeathed the whole thing to his old college – Magdalene, in Cambridge – where construction of a new library building was already nearly complete. Pepys' books, including the manuscript of his *Diary*, were installed here in 1724.

PLATE 41

THE GATEWAY OF TRINITY COLLEGE

High up on the front of the massive Great Gate, a memorial to the college's founder also
commemorates a venerable Cambridge tradition – that of the undergraduate prank.

The dignified statue of King Henry VIII, who
founded Trinity – Cambridge's richest college –
stands in pride of place above the archways of the
Great Gate and has presided over the ceremonial
admission of a long succession of distinguished
gentlemen to the post of Master. A close
look at it reveals a surprise, however:
the king's right hand holds aloft a
chair leg, put there many years ago
as an incongruous replacement
for his sceptre. In the 1980s the
joke was taken a stage further and for a short
while a bicycle pump appeared there instead.
The college authorities apparently felt this
was going a little bit too far, so it was removed
and the chair leg was reinstated.

In the seventeenth century an arcaded building
to the right of the Great Gate housed the revered
Lucasian Professor, Sir Isaac Newton, who for thirty years had a
private laboratory here with its own enclosed garden.

Wills's
Cigarettes.

VIRTUS VERA NOBILITAS

Arms of
Trinity College
Cambridge University

ARMS OF
OXFORD & CAMBRIDGE COLLEGES
A SERIES OF 42. No 18
WILLS'S CIGARETTES
TRINITY COLLEGE, CAMBRIDGE.

Michelhouse, Cambridge, was founded in
1324 by Hervey of Stanton, Chancellor of the
Exchequer in the reign of Edward II. King's
Hall, Cambridge, was founded in 1337 by King
Edward III., in furtherance of an uncompleted
plan of his father's. King Henry VIII. amalgamated these two foundations, very largely
increased them, and in 1546 founded one magnificent College, which he dedicated to the
Holy and Undivided Trinity. Queen Mary
afterwards added twenty Scholarships. The
Mastership of this College is in the Gift of the
Crown. The Arms, which show the Royal
Lion of England, were first recorded in 1572,
but there is reason to think they may really
date back to the foundation of the College.

W.D & H.O WILLS. Bristol & London
ISSUED BY THE IMPERIAL TOBACCO COMPANY
(OF GREAT BRITAIN & IRELAND), LIMITED.

PLATE 42

THE GREAT COURT, TRINITY COLLEGE

Trinity College owes its existence to Catherine Parr, the wise and capable
sixth wife of Henry VIII, and its beauty to Thomas Nevile, its great Elizabethan Master.

After dissolving the monasteries, King Henry turned his attention to the colleges. The University authorities, much alarmed, approached the Queen. She took up their cause, and persuaded her husband that what Cambridge really needed was a grand new college with him as its honoured Founder. Rather than paying for it all himself, however, he dissolved two existing colleges, King's Hall and Michaelhouse, and closed seven hostels. Adding the resources of these foundations to the money derived from dissolved monasteries provided the basis for the University's richest college.

In the words of George Macaulay Trevelyan, "If Henry VIII founded Trinity, Nevile built it." Thomas Nevile became Master in 1593 and inherited a miscellaneous collection of buildings. King's Gate, for example — shown on the left in the painting — had been the entrance to King's Hall. Over the next decade he demolished some buildings, moved others brick by brick to new locations, and imposed order and harmony upon the whole project. Great Court, the largest college courtyard in England, is his magnificent achievement.

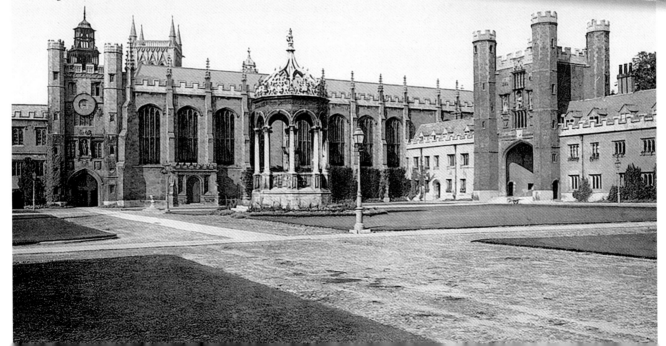

PLATE 43

THE HALL OF TRINITY COLLEGE FROM NEVILE'S COURT

The main part of this court – where Lord Byron had his rooms when
he was a student – was Dr Thomas Nevile's final gift to his college.

Dr Nevile, Master of the college until his death in 1615, used his own money for the construction of this much-admired court on the western side of the Hall. It is the most sought-after location within Trinity: there is more competition among Fellows and undergraduates for the rooms here than for those in any other part of the college.

The north cloister of the court, shown on the left in the painting, is the place where Isaac Newton, the most illustrious Fellow in the history of the college, first determined the speed of sound – by stamping his foot and timing the resulting echo.

During the First World War the cloisters of Nevile's Court were curtained off and transformed into a field hospital, the First Eastern General Hospital, for wounded soldiers. They made a poignant contrast with the healthy young men who were to be seen at the same time in Great Court, being drilled as soldiers before being sent overseas to take their place in the fighting.

Plan of the older parts of Trinity College

1 Bishop's Hostel
2 Nevile's Gate
3 Site of Garret Hostl
4 Sundial
5 Master's Garden
6 Bowling Green
7 King's Hall Cloister

–1546, Remains of King's Hall
1546–1592
1592–1615. In Nevile's Mastership
1670–1774
1823–1893

PLATE 44

NEVILE'S GATE, TRINITY COLLEGE

The academic life of the colleges could not have been carried on without
the practical support of a great many servants and tradesmen.

Archbold Marshall, writing in 1899, described Trinity's Great Court on a typical termtime morning, when most undergraduates would have been out attending lectures or studying: "Its chief occupants appear to be the bed-makers, who empty their pails down the gratings, or stand for a few minutes' gossip by their respective staircases. Every now and then an idler passes through in a leisurely manner, or a don scurries across the grass in a terrible hurry. White-aproned cooks from the college kitchens collect plate and crockery from the various gyp-rooms and carry them away in green boxes balanced on their heads. Tradesmen's boys, their baskets on their arms, pass from one staircase to another."

The college kitchens are shown on the left in this painting; Great Court is on the other side of them. The gate that gives access to Trinity Lane was originally constructed as a riverside entrance for Nevile's Court. It was moved to its present location when the Wren Library was built.

TRINITY COLLEGE BRIDGE AND AVENUE, WITH GATE LEADING INTO THE NEW COURT

New Court, designed by William Watkins in 1825 in the Tudor-Gothic style that was fashionable at the time, provided much-needed extra student rooms for Trinity College.

Trinity College expanded greatly during the nineteenth century, when it led the University's reformation and was home to many leading scholars and scientists. Christopher Wordsworth (brother of the poet), who was Master at the time, built New Court in order to reduce the number of undergraduates who were exposed to the temptations of the town by being forced to live outside the college in lodging-houses.

Sir Arthur Conan Doyle brought fiction's most famous detective, Sherlock Holmes, to Cambridge in 1904 in *The Adventure of the Missing Three-Quarter*. Holmes is called in by the captain of the Varsity rugby team, a Trinity undergraduate, to find a player who has disappeared, and visits several nearby villages in the course of his investigation.

Like many similar English pleasure grounds, the gardens of the Backs were devastated by Dutch elm disease in the twentieth century. The magnificent trees shown in this painting were planted in the 1670s, but have since been replaced with limes and flowering cherries.

PLATE 46

CAIUS COLLEGE AND THE SENATE HOUSE FROM ST MARY'S PASSAGE

Undergraduates at Gonville and Caius may be remembered for their inventive pranks and rags, many involving the neighbouring Senate House.

Strongly discouraged by the authorities at Caius College, because it is extremely dangerous for any student attempting it, is the notorious "Senate House Leap", a leap across the narrow passage between Caius and the Senate House with a drop of nearly thirty metres below. The starting point is a window in one of the turret rooms, a convenient feature provided by Alfred Waterhouse when he adopted a French Renaissance style for his 1870s college extension.

Other stunts are now remembered with more affection, though they were not approved of at the time. The one widely credited with starting an honourable tradition is the feat achieved soon after the First World War by a team who captured a 6-ton artillery piece that had been on display in the town and smuggled it into Caius Court under cover of darkness. This feat was spectacularly topped in 1958 by a group of engineers who managed, in one night and with no damage to the fabric of the building, to install an Austin Seven van (minus its engine) on the apex of the Senate House roof.

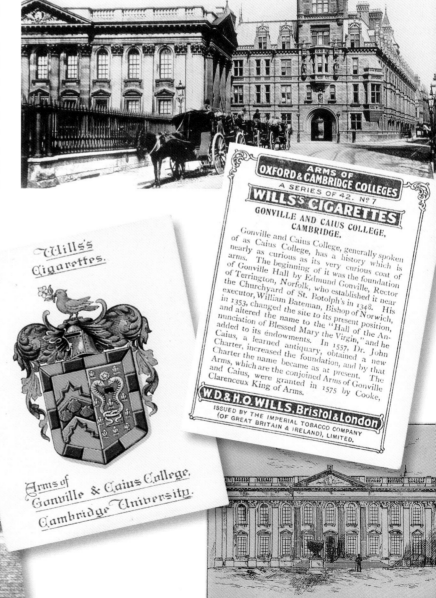

ARMS OF
OXFORD & CAMBRIDGE COLLEGES
A SERIES OF 42. Nº 7

WILL'S CIGARETTES

GONVILLE AND CAIUS COLLEGE,
CAMBRIDGE.

Gonville and Caius College, generally spoken of as Caius College, has a history which is nearly as curious as its very curious coat of arms. The beginning of it was the foundation of Gonville Hall by Edmund Gonville, Rector of Terrington, Norfolk, who established it near the Churchyard of St. Botolph's in 1348. His executor, William Bateman, Bishop of Norwich, in 1353, changed the site to its present position, and altered the name to the "Hall of the Annunciation of Blessed Mary the Virgin," and he added to its endowments. In 1557, Dr. John Caius, a learned antiquary, obtained a new Charter, increased the foundation, and by that Charter the name became as at present. The Arms, which are the conjoined Arms of Gonville and Caius, were granted in 1575 by Cooke, Clarenceux King of Arms.

W.D.& H.O.WILLS, Bristol & London
ISSUED BY THE IMPERIAL TOBACCO COMPANY
(OF GREAT BRITAIN & IRELAND), LIMITED.

Will's
Cigarettes.

Arms of
Gonville & Caius College,
Cambridge University.

PLATE 47

THE GATE OF VIRTUE, GONVILLE AND CAIUS COLLEGE

The Gates of Virtue and Honour, built during the reign of Elizabeth I when Caius extended the medieval Gonville Hall, are remarkably early examples of Classical architecture in England.

Dr Keys, a sixteenth-century physician and a graduate of Gonville Hall, latinised his name to Caius during a sojourn at Padua University in Italy, which explains why the college's name is pronounced "Keys". After returning to England he came back to his old college, refounding and extending it. The court he built, Caius Court, is interesting architecturally because its general design is in the standard style for the period, but he provided a complete contrast by adding the classical gates. It is thought that he had a hand in designing them personally, and that they were inspired by French and Italian buildings rather than by anything in England.

The openness of the southern side of the court – it is closed only by a wall, not by a range of buildings – is another example of Caius' progressive thinking. It was intended to improve the ventilation of the buildings "lest the air from being confined within a narrow space should become foul".

Cambridge, Caius College, Gate of Virtue

PLATE 48

THE GATE OF HONOUR, CAIUS COLLEGE

When Dr Caius named the three classical gates of his college, he had in mind a
symbolic progression that would contribute to the students' moral education.

The plan was that students would enter Gonville and
Caius College by the Gate of Humility, which
was originally at the front entrance on Trinity
Street (though it was moved in the nineteenth
century). They would then pass through the
Gate of Virtue, which gives access to Caius
Court, and finally leave via the Gate of Honour
on their way to receive their degrees. Honour
could only be attained by way of Virtue.

For the first century and a half after
the Gate of Honour was built, the
destination of the graduation-day
procession would have been Great St
Mary's Church. Once the Senate House had been
built the ceremony was relocated there, giving the
Caius students an even shorter distance to walk.

The building visible beyond the Gate of
Honour to the right, the Cockrell Building, was
constructed as the main University Library, a
role it fulfilled until the present one was built,
after which it was used for the Law Library.
It has now been taken over by Caius as the
College's working library.

Gate of Honour & Gate of
Virtue. Caius College

W. Matthison

PLATE 49

THE FIRST COURT
OF EMMANUEL COLLEGE

Sir Christopher Wren's much-admired new chapel on the northern side
of Front Court gave an elegant new look to the college.

Emmanuel was founded during the reign of Elizabeth I by her Chancellor of the Exchequer, Sir Walter Mildmay, reusing buildings from a Dominican priory that had flourished alongside Cambridge's early colleges until Henry VIII dissolved it.

In the seventeenth century some of the old monastic buildings were deemed to be unsatisfactory, and the Master invited a young architect, Christopher Wren, to design a new chapel. Wren created a replacement for the entire northern range of the court, with an arcaded passageway and above it a Long Gallery, intended as a reception room where the Master and his guests could also take a walk for exercise in bad weather (the "little ice age" was under way at the time, so provision for bad weather must have been an important consideration). The chapel itself begins behind the gallery, though Wren's clever design makes it appear to front onto the court.

PLATE 50

THE OLD COURT IN EMMANUEL COLLEGE

While studying at Emmanuel, John Harvard occupied a dormer-windowed room overlooking the large stained-glass window of the Hall, a building that had been the Dominicans' chapel before the college was founded.

Sir Walter Mildmay, Emmanuel's founder, intended his college as a training ground for Protestant clergymen – though he gave an equivocal answer when Queen Elizabeth I accused him of going too far in that direction and creating a Puritan foundation: "No, Madam, far be it from me to countenance anything contrary to your established laws, but I have set an acorn, which when it becomes an oak, God alone knows what will be the fruit thereof."

In the following century some of these fruits became apparent: of the thirteen new heads of Cambridge colleges who were appointed under

Oliver Cromwell, seven were members of Emmanuel; and of the first hundred University graduates to settle in New England, a third came from this college. Notable among these graduates was John Harvard, who went on to found a new college in Cambridge, Massachusetts, that still bears his name.

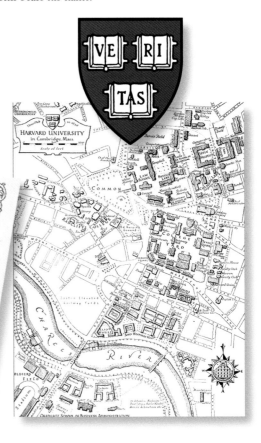

PLATE 51

THE LAKE AND NEW BUILDINGS, EMMANUEL COLLEGE

The lake in the grounds of Emmanuel has been there longer than the college itself:
it was once the fishpond of the great Dominican priory that previously occupied the site.

The paddock around the lake once had a practical purpose as a home for the Fellows' horses, and a brewhouse stood beyond it. Now the paddock is valued as a garden, and the late-Victorian building, called the Hostel, that replaced the brewhouse provides accommodation for undergraduates. It was designed by the well-meaning college authorities as an affordable home for those of modest means who might not otherwise be able to study at Cambridge, and therefore has smaller rooms than those in the rest of the college.

Thomas Young, a member of the college at the end of the eighteenth century, was one of the world's true polymaths, making significant contributions in a wide range of fields including music, optics, medicine and linguistics. He is said to have been inspired to develop his experiments that led to the wave theory of light by the patterns of ripples that the swans produced on the surface of Emmanuel's lake.

PLATE 52

THE CLOISTER COURT,
SIDNEY SUSSEX COLLEGE

The ornate range along the eastern side of Cloister Court, built in 1890, was the last word
in late-Victorian sophistication; the mullioned window of the Elizabethan Hall can be seen to the right of it.

This is one of the few parts of Sidney Sussex where red-brick
walls are still visible. Most of the college's buildings had them
originally, but the first two courts were extensively remodelled
in the 1820s in a variation of the Gothic style, with battlements
added and the brickwork covered with cement facings, to create
an appearance rather like that of a castle. The result was not
greatly admired by later generations.

The college, like Emmanuel, had been set up as a Puritan
establishment during the reign of Elizabeth I, reusing a site
that had belonged to one of the Catholic religious houses
– in Sidney's case, a Fransiscan friary. This had co-existed
with the earlier colleges in Cambridge until Henry VIII
dissolved it. It was intended by its founder, Frances Sidney,
the Countess of Sussex, for the training of Church of
England clergymen; one of its earliest students
was Oliver Cromwell.

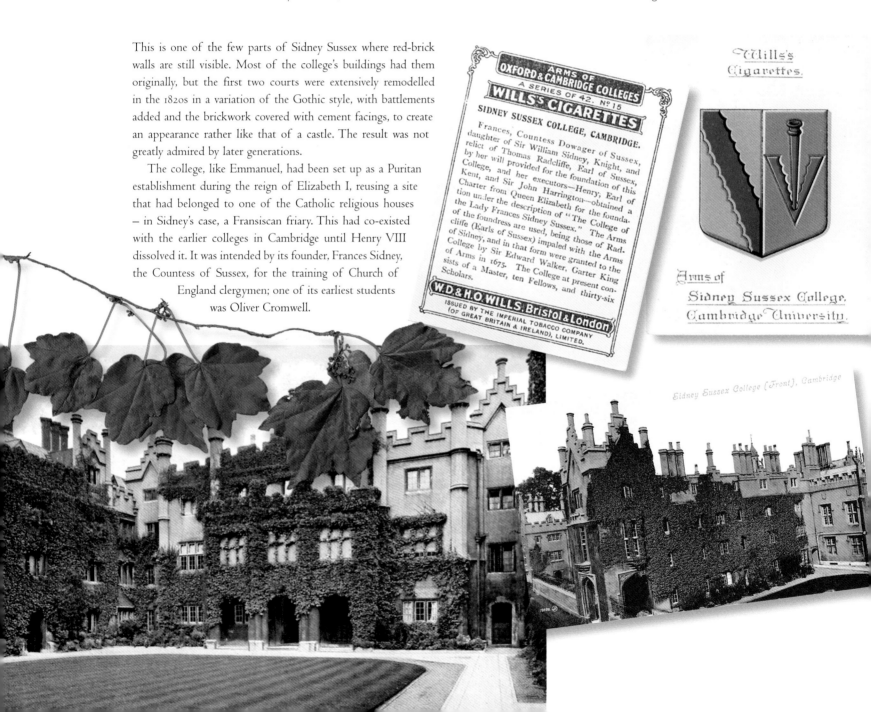

ARMS OF
OXFORD & CAMBRIDGE COLLEGES
A SERIES OF 42. No 15
WILL'S CIGARETTES
SIDNEY SUSSEX COLLEGE, CAMBRIDGE.

Frances, Countess Dowager of Sussex,
daughter of Sir William Sidney, Knight, and
relict of Thomas Radcliffe, Earl of Sussex,
by her will provided for the foundation of this
College, and her executors—Henry, Earl of
Kent, and Sir John Harrington—obtained a
Charter from Queen Elizabeth for the foundation under the description of "The College of
the Lady Frances Sidney Sussex." The Arms
of the foundress are used, being those of Radcliffe (Earls of Sussex) impaled with the Arms
of Sidney, and in that form were granted to the
College by Sir Edward Walker, Garter King
of Arms in 1675. The College at present consists of a Master, ten Fellows, and thirty-six
Scholars.

W.D.&H.O.WILLS, Bristol & London
ISSUED BY THE IMPERIAL TOBACCO COMPANY
(OF GREAT BRITAIN & IRELAND), LIMITED.

Wills's
Cigarettes.

Arms of
Sidney Sussex College,
Cambridge University.

Sidney Sussex College (Front), Cambridge

PLATE 53

DOWNING COLLEGE FROM THE ENTRANCE IN REGENT STREET

Downing was the only new college to be founded in Cambridge between 1594 and 1869,
and its founding was something of an accident.

The money to build this college came from the fortune of Sir George Downing (who also built Downing Street in London) via his grandson, who left it in his 1749 will to a succession of four cousins. If all of them died without having produced children, the money was to be used to found a Cambridge college.

As it turned out, none of the four cousins did have children, but the foundation of the college was severely delayed when the widow of one of them refused to give up the estate. The resulting legal battle dragged on until 1800, its expenses eventually consuming a large part of the money.

The result was that only part of the grand neoclassical court that had been planned could be built. The east and west ranges were constructed, facing one another across a large expanse of garden. The north side was built in the 1950s, and the court still remains open along its southern edge.

Wills's Cigarettes.

QUÆRERE VERUM

Arms of
Downing College.
Cambridge University

ARMS OF
OXFORD & CAMBRIDGE COLLEGES
A SERIES OF 42. No 5
WILL'S CIGARETTES
DOWNING COLLEGE, CAMBRIDGE.

This College owes its foundation to Sir George Downing, of Gamlingay Park, Co. Cambridge, Baronet and Knight of the Bath, who by his will dated Dec. 20, 1717, created an ultimate remainder to build and found a College in the University. It was not until 1764 that the life-interests created by the will lapsed; but further litigation ensued, and it was not until Sept. 22, 1800, that the Great Seal was affixed to the Charter of Foundation which incorporated the College with the University. The statutes provide that the College shall consist of a Master, two Professors, six Fellows, and at least six Scholars. The Arms are those of the founder within a bordure, and were granted to the College April 18, 1801.

W.D.&H.O. WILLS, Bristol & London
ISSUED BY THE IMPERIAL TOBACCO COMPANY
(OF GREAT BRITAIN & IRELAND), LIMITED.

Cambridge, Downing Colle

PLATE 54

TRUMPINGTON STREET FROM PETERHOUSE

Pembroke College's Red Buildings, designed in the 1870s by Alfred Waterhouse,
are to the right of this painting. The Pitt Press is in the distance on the opposite side of the road.

The tower of the Pitt Press building on Trumpington Street, home of Cambridge University Press, resembles that of a church – it was commonly called by Edwardian undergraduates "the freshers' church", as new students sometimes mistook it for one. The building is named in honour of William Pitt the Younger, who had been educated just across the road at Pembroke. It was constructed using surplus funds when, after his death, a collection to pay for a statue raised far more money than was needed for that purpose.

The University Press, which operates under a charter first granted by Henry VIII, is the oldest printing and publishing house in the world, and continues to be a leader in academic and educational titles. It is still a department of the University, not an independent company, and like other such concerns – the University Library and the Botanic Garden, for example – it is managed by a University Syndicate.

PITT PRESS.

W. Mathison

PLATE 55

PEASHILL

Peas Hill (as it is known today), just off the Market Square, probably derives its name from the Latin word "piscaria" or fish market. There had been fish stalls here for centuries.

This street is not really a hill, of course. Cambridge's "hills" were just patches of firmer ground that originally stood slightly above the marshy land around them. The difference in level disappeared long ago as the marshy areas were filled in, but one relic of it remains in the continued existence of huge ancient cellars. These were used by the inns for storing wine, and there is a rumour that they connect up and join with an underground passage that continues along Trinity Street as far as the Round Church.

Peas Hill was to undergo a great transformation in the twentieth century. A corner of the Guildhall now stands on the site of the Bell Inn, and the entrance to the Arts Theatre is opposite it. The old town pump, which was still in use for washing out fish boxes as late as 1914, is now gone, but the remains of the smaller pump beside it survive.

Market Day, Cambridge.

PLATE 56

OLD HOUSES NEAR ST EDWARD'S CHURCH AND ST EDWARD'S PASSAGE

This charming passageway between Peas Hill and King's Parade has long been
a favourite haunt for lovers of books, music and the stage.

David's Bookshop, still in business today just behind St Edward's Church, started life as a stall on the market round the corner. The young John Maynard Keynes, who graduated from King's College in 1905, was a great devotee of this bookstall, and would often appear on Friday evenings to help Mr David unpack the newly arrived books for display, so as to get first sight of them.

Thirty years later, when he was Bursar of King's, Keynes was to make his mark on St Edward's Passage in a more lasting way. He was the person who realised that a full-size theatre would fit into the space available between the existing buildings if certain compromises were made – for example, if the conventional notion that a theatre must have a rectangular stage could be dispensed with. The Arts Theatre, with its front entrance in Peas Hill and its stage door in St Edward's Passage, rapidly became a Cambridge institution.

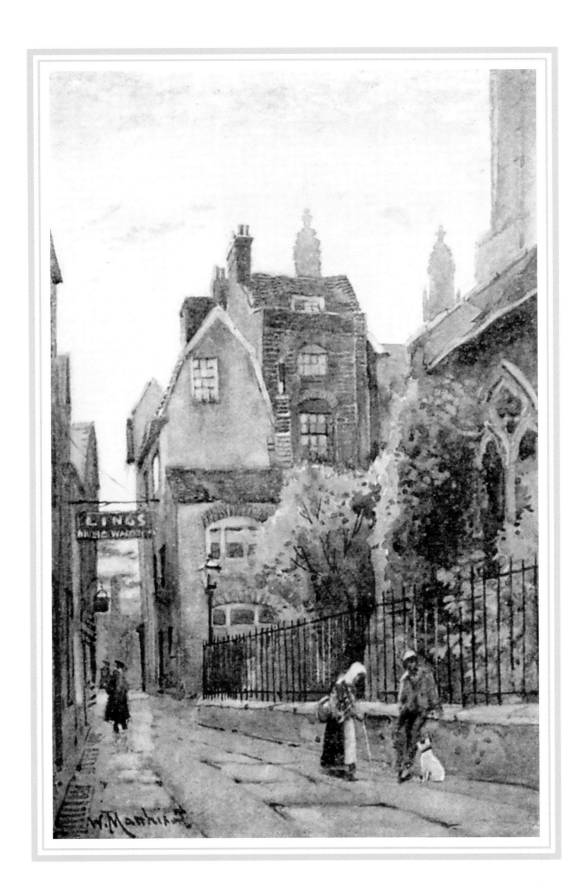

PLATE 57

MARKET STREET AND HOLY TRINITY CHURCH

Market Street, the shopping centre of Cambridge, was in the early twentieth century home
to the town's two premier department stores, both long-established family-run businesses.

Joshua Taylor's store was a relative newcomer to the town, having opened in Sidney Street in 1860. In 1900 it added a bootmaking, tailoring and outfitting department in the grand building on the corner of Market Street, opposite Holy Trinity Church – thus becoming part of a tradition dating from the Middle Ages, when Market Street had been known as Shoemaker Lane.

Eaden Lilley's business was founded in 1750 a little further down Market Street towards Great St Mary's Church. It began as a haberdashery and grew into a huge and varied enterprise selling everything from groceries to furniture.

The junction of Market and Sidney Streets was one of the busiest in town, particularly after August 1907 when the newly-formed Ortona Motor Company introduced a popular bus service that ran from the railway station via Sidney Street to New Chesterton. A one-way traffic system was introduced here in 1927.

PLATE 58

GREAT ST MARY'S, FROM TRINITY STREET

The tower of the University church is visible at the southern
end of Trinity Street, where it joins King's Parade.

Trinity Street, though narrow, was bustling in the early twentieth century – especially during termtime. Early in the morning college servants would have been a common sight, walking down the street with breakfast trays balanced on their heads for undergraduates who were living in the lodging houses here. The street's main landlord is Trinity College, and most of the shops served the needs of academic customers in one way or another. They included tailors and gentlemen's outfitters, a grocery, hairdressers, several bookshops, banks, and Hobbs' sporting equipment store, which was run by the brother of the famous Cambridge-born cricketer. At the far end of the street, opposite Great St Mary's Church, Number 1 Trinity Street is the oldest bookshop in the country. It is remembered as the building in the famous 1897 photograph of a female effigy on a bicycle, taken during one of the votes on whether the University should grant degrees to women.

PLATE 59

THE LAKE IN THE BOTANIC GARDENS

The University Botanic Garden has always had a serious scientific purpose,
though generations of visitors from both "town" and "gown" have also appreciated it for its beauty.

The first Botanic Garden in Cambridge, a formal physic garden, was established in 1762 on the land where the lecture rooms and laboratories of the New Museums Site now stand. The current garden was the brainchild of Professor John Stevens Henslow, the teacher who first inspired Charles Darwin to study natural history. It opened to the public in 1846. Henslow was particularly interested in trees, which he regarded as the world's most important plants, and he established his garden on a large site where there was space for a considerable collection from all over the world – including the oldest giant redwoods in Britain.

Much of the planting in the garden is arranged on scientific principles, with many of the plants, including trees, grouped into biological families, so that their relationships and differences can be studied. Beauty, however, has not been neglected, and the garden is also a delightful retreat.

PLATE 60

PARKER'S PIECE

As well as being the venue for feasts and festivals, this green space has
played a significant part in the history of two traditional English sports.

Cricket has been played on Parker's Piece
since 1831, when an area was levelled for
the purpose – and played
most famously by Jack
Hobbs, who was England's
foremost batsman for
thirty years
from 1905.
Hobbs was born in
Cambridge, where his father was on
the staff of the University cricket
ground, and the boy learned to
play on the Piece.

This park is also the place
where the "Cambridge Rules" for
football made their first appearance,
a crucial step in the development
of Association Football.

Parker's Piece has belonged to the town
since 1613, when it was obtained from Trinity
College in exchange for the land where the
Wren Library now stands (Parker was the
tenant farmer who was renting it from Trinity at
the time). It has hosted numerous great public
events, including a dinner for 15,000 guests to
celebrate Queen Victoria's coronation and the rather
smaller one seventy years later to mark that of
Edward VII.

Parker's Pieces, Parkside, Cambridge

47385.

PLATE 61

TRINITY BRIDGE, KING'S COLLEGE CHAPEL IN THE DISTANCE

The bank of the river, as it winds past the backs of Trinity College, Trinity Hall,
Clare and King's, is a favourite place for a stroll.

Trinity Bridge, designed by James Essex in the mid-eighteenth century, was funded by a bequest of £1,500 from a Dr Francis Hooper. His coat of arms is carved on its side along with that of the college.

The swans on the Cam are much appreciated for their beauty by visitors and residents alike. The Master and Fellows of St John's College are also permitted to appreciate them in a different way: they have a royal licence that enables them to serve roast swan at their feasts – a privilege that, elsewhere in the country, belongs either to the Crown or to two of the City of London Livery Companies.

Unusually for Matthison's work, the view shown in this painting is not entirely accurate. In reality the buildings of Trinity Hall are more prominent than they appear to be here, and they conceal more of King's Chapel.

2947. TRINITY COLLEGE BRIDGE, CAMBRIDGE

PLATE 62

THE TOWER OF ST JOHN'S
COLLEGE CHAPEL FROM THE RIVER

The view downstream along the river at the backs of Trinity
and St John's Colleges is one of the most admired in Cambridge.

Thames-style pleasure punts were introduced to Cambridge, as an alternative to the canoes, rowing-boats and square-ended garden punts then popular, at the beginning of the twentieth century. In Cambridge the person propelling a punt stands up on the deck at the stern, rather than lower down in the boat as is usual in Oxford. Tradition has it that this custom arose here because of punting's popularity with ladies, who found it easier to manage the puntpole from this position.

Just visible on the right of the painting is Trinity College's library, a magnificent building by Sir Christopher Wren, which houses many important documents including, because A.A. Milne was educated at Trinity, the original 1926 manuscript of *Winnie-the-Pooh*. The library is practical as well as beautiful: there are long rows of high windows on each side with bookcases beneath, maximising the available light for study.

St John's College Chapel, disproportionately large, dominates the view from every direction.

PLATE 63

UNIVERSITY BOAT-HOUSES
ON THE CAM – SUNSET

Downstream of the colleges the river was used, as it still is today, for both rowing and fishing.

The University had acquired a taste for active sports, especially rowing, in Victorian times, and by 1900 many college-based clubs had built boathouses on the north bank of the river. The painting shows Emmanuel's boathouse, with those of Pembroke and Clare visible through the trees beyond it. They faced the green space of Midsummer Common, whose tree-lined bank remained popular with both "town" and "gown" for more sedentary pursuits such as fishing.

In the Edwardian era a new middle-class quarter of Cambridge, New Chesterton, was growing up behind the long row of college boathouses. It consisted of rows of trim villas, each with a pocket-handkerchief-sized front garden, in streets with names like Kimberley and Pretoria that were so well known during the Boer War. Connecting this suburb with the town were several passenger ferries – the one shown in the painting was called the Cutter Ferry or Dant's Ferry – which were pulled across the river on chains. They were later replaced by footbridges.

Old Chesterton Ferry, Cambridge

PLATE 64

DITTON CORNER, ON THE CAM

The pretty village of Fen Ditton, on the River Cam a little way downstream
of Cambridge, is well known to the town's rowing enthusiasts.

The peace of the riverside meadows is disturbed for a few days
each summer by enthusiastic crowds of spectators who descend
on Fen Ditton to watch the oarsmen (and nowadays oarswomen)
competing in the May Races, or "Bumps". This tradition began
in Victorian times and has remained hugely popular ever since.
Ditton Corner is an especially valued vantage point because
it gives a good view of the action. The sharp bend here often
gives rise to a "bump" – the exciting moment at which a chasing
crew makes contact with the one in front and its victory is
acknowledged.

A "grind" ferry – one pulled across the river on chains – that
connected the Chesterton bank to the Plough Inn at Fen Ditton
was the scene of a serious accident during the 1905 May Races.
A group of undergraduates forced
themselves onto the already full ferry,
which overturned, and three women
were drowned.

CAMBRIDGE, 1910.

PLATE 65

THE FITZWILLIAM MUSEUM – EVENING

The collections of Cambridge University's museum have been enriched by donations
from many art-lovers, making it one of the best in the country.

The imposing neoclassical building in Trumpington Street was built to house the huge personal art collection that had been amassed by Richard, Seventh Viscount Fitzwilliam of Merrion, after he bequeathed it to the University in 1816. As a collector from the age of the Grand Tour he naturally concentrated on Renaissance art: the museum therefore began its existence with an impressive catalogue of paintings including works by Titian, Veronese and Palma Vecchio, and a magnificent collection of etchings including a great many by Rembrandt.

During the nineteenth century, collectors developed a taste for medieval art and also bought new work by their own contemporaries such as the Impressionists and the Pre-Raphaelites. Many such collectors gave or bequeathed their treasures to the Fitzwilliam, and it now contains important artworks from all periods of history, from ancient Egypt, Greece and Rome to the present day.

Cambridge. Fitzwilliam Museum. Front.

PLATE 66

UNIVERSITY CHURCH OF GREAT ST MARY

Great St Mary's (as it is known today) has been the University's church,
as well as being the largest parish church in the town, since the Middle Ages.

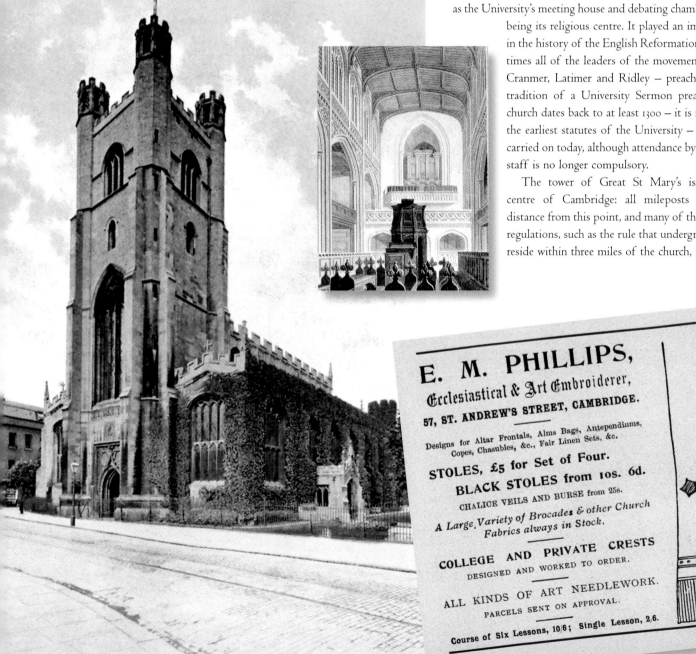

Until the Senate House was built for the purpose in the eighteenth century, Great St Mary's was used for degree ceremonies and served as the University's meeting house and debating chamber, as well as being its religious centre. It played an important part in the history of the English Reformation: at different times all of the leaders of the movement – Erasmus, Cranmer, Latimer and Ridley – preached here. The tradition of a University Sermon preached in this church dates back to at least 1300 – it is mentioned in the earliest statutes of the University – and it is still carried on today, although attendance by students and staff is no longer compulsory.

The tower of Great St Mary's is the official centre of Cambridge: all mileposts measure the distance from this point, and many of the University's regulations, such as the rule that undergraduates must reside within three miles of the church, relate to it.

PLATE 67

ADDENBROOKE'S HOSPITAL IN TRUMPINGTON STREET

Sir Matthew Digby Wyatt's imposing building housed the Cambridge General Hospital for more than a century.

Dr John Addenbrooke, who had been Bursar of St Catharine's College and a London physician, died in 1719 leaving his fortune of £4,500 (subject to his wife's life interest) to be spent on the foundation of a "small physicall hospital for poor people". Addenbrooke's Hospital, one of the first Voluntary General Hospitals outside London, opened to patients in 1766. It was supported for almost two centuries by bequests and subscriptions until it was incorporated into the National Health Service in 1948.

The original building in Trumpington Street was remodelled in 1864–5 by the architect Sir Matthew Digby Wyatt, and survived serious fires in 1902 and 1906. Work began on the much larger New Addenbrooke's site on the edge of the city almost a century later, but the last patients were not moved out of the old hospital until 1984.

In the 1990s Old Addenbrooke's underwent a startling transformation, and the building, its façade redecorated in glowing colours, now houses the Judge Business School.

PLATE 68

THE GREAT BRIDGE – BRIDGE STREET

From the earliest times Cambridge was a significant crossroads, as it was both an inland port and a river crossing.

As its name suggests, the town of Cambridge came into existence around a river crossing – one certainly used by the Romans (today's Huntingdon Road was part of the Via Devana, leading from Colchester through Godmanchester to Chester) and probably by earlier travellers too. The cast-iron Great Bridge, dating from 1823 and the latest in a succession of structures on the site, is today called Magdalene Bridge after the college beside it.

Cambridge was also an important inland port at a time when all heavy goods had to be moved by water, before the coming of the railways. The wharves and hythes in their heyday took up most of the riverbank, including the area now occupied by college gardens, but by the early twentieth century commercial river traffic had declined and was mostly confined to the area around the Great Bridge.

Many warehouse buildings, still in use in 1907, have since been converted into cafés and restaurants. Magdalene College, no longer hidden behind trees, now shows its face to the river.

PLATE 69

VIEW OF CAMBRIDGE
FROM THE CASTLE HILL

The top of Cambridge's only hill, conveniently close to the river crossing that gave
the town its name, has been the location preferred by anyone who needed to build a castle.

There was a defended enclosure on Castle Hill in the Iron Age;
the ancient Romans replaced it with a fortress, probably wooden,
and the Normans built a stone castle. This survived many years
of extensions and improvements and was last used during the
Civil War. Its gatehouse had a long afterlife as a prison, but was
eventually demolished by the Victorians who reused the stone to
construct a purpose-built gaol and courthouse.

The view from the top of the hill is dominated by the tower of
St John's College Chapel, with King's Chapel visible to the right.
The church in the foreground, that of St Giles, was rebuilt in the
nineteenth century on the site of a much more ancient one.

In Edwardian times there was great poverty in Castle End, the
area around the castle site, which had a reputation as the town's red
light district. It was notorious for its tumbledown cottages, from
which gangs of rough boys would throw stones at passers-by.

PLATE 70

GIRTON COLLEGE – EVENING

England's first residential college for women moved into the village of Girton, two miles outside Cambridge, in 1873, with the intention of becoming a full part of the University.

Girton's visionary founder, Emily Davies, had always aimed at complete equality for her students. She would have no compromise with "lectures for ladies" and the special examinations, at a lower level than the University's Tripos, that were offered to them. At the beginning it was very hard to find students who were well enough prepared because the standard of teaching at girls' schools was not high, but Miss Davies was determined.

By the end of the Victorian era, Girton College was comfortably established in a fine red-brick building, designed by Alfred Waterhouse and standing in spacious grounds. It had its traditions, its college songs, its hockey team, and even its own volunteer fire brigade – set up by students five years after the college was built, and carried on by them for many years with great dedication – but at the time Matthison painted this scene it was still campaigning for official recognition as a college of the University.

PLATE 71

THE BOATHOUSE ON
ROBINSON CRUSOE'S ISLAND

An excursion by rowing boat on the upper river, above Cambridge, was a favourite pastime
for both ladies and gentlemen – though it was not without its embarrassing moments.

The stretch of river above the town had always been relatively clean, even before the introduction of proper drainage in the 1890s made boating pleasant along the Backs. The Victorian upper classes still had some problems to face, however, when setting off towards Grantchester with their picnic baskets. Unfortunately for their sense of propriety, the river was not only popular for boating.

Gwen Raverat, who was taken on many such excursions as a child, described their difficulties in her memoirs many years later: "All summer, Sheep's Green and Coe Fen were pink with boys, as naked as God made them; for bathing drawers did not exist then; or, at least, not on Sheep's Green. To go Up the River, the goal of all the best picnics, the boats had to go right by the bathing places, which lay on both sides of the narrow stream. The Gentlemen were set to the oars, and each Lady unfurled a parasol, and, like an ostrich, buried her head in it."

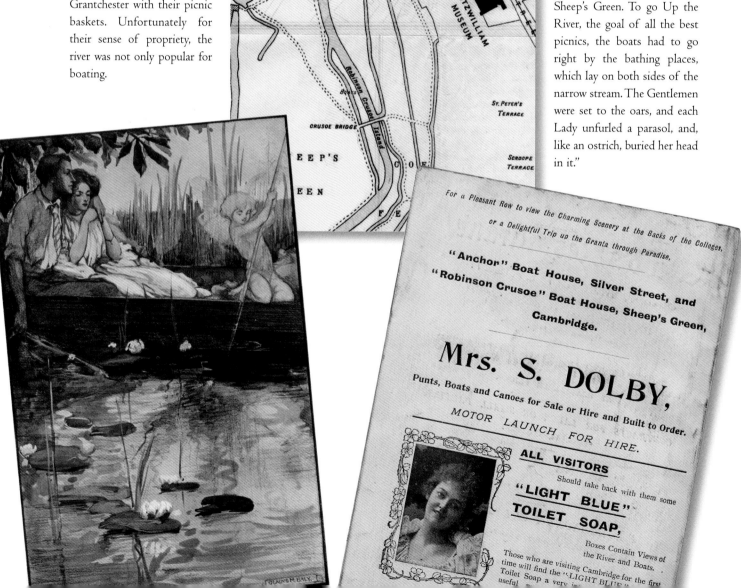

PLATE 72

QUEENS' LANE – THE SITE OF THE OLD MILL STREET

In gaining its most famous monument, King's College Chapel, Cambridge lost one of its principal streets.
The remaining parts of it survive as quiet lanes.

Mill Street (sometimes called Milne Street) was one of the main thoroughfares of the town until 1443, when King Henry VI conceived a grand plan. His vision of a new college with a huge and magnificent chapel could only be realised by sweeping away a large part of the existing medieval town, and Mill Street in particular had to go because it ran right through the middle of the site on which he wanted to build.

Ever since then the two severed halves of Mill Street, now known as Queens' Lane and Trinity Lane, have been charming lanes whose only purpose is to give access to the college and University gateways that still line the street: the main entrances of Queens' College, Clare College, the Old Schools and Trinity Hall, and Nevile's Gate at Trinity College. Until the eighteenth century the main gate of St Catharine's College was also in Mill Street.

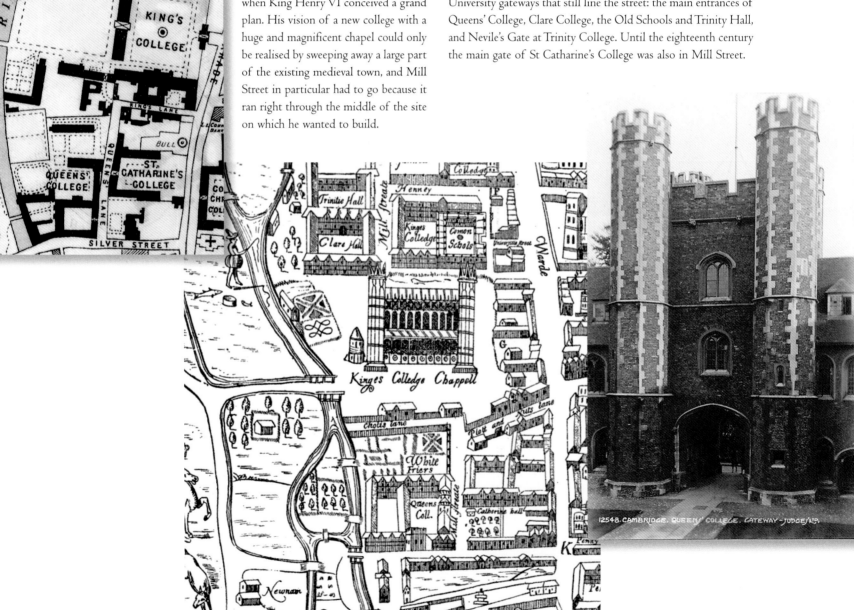

12548. CAMBRIDGE. QUEENS' COLLEGE. GATEWAY – JUDGES LD.

PLATE 73

MERTON HALL

The School of Pythagoras, the oldest domestic dwelling in Cambridge,
was for many centuries owned by an Oxford college.

Merton Hall, which stands at the western edge of St John's College and now belongs to it, was originally built in about 1200 as a private house. Very few houses this old survive in Britain. Its owner, Richard Dunning, sold it to Merton College, Oxford, in 1271, when the beginnings of a University already existed in Cambridge but its first college had not yet been founded. It remained the property of Merton College for nearly seven hundred years.

The oldest section of the building is the stone part at the southern end, which began at some point to be called the School of Pythagoras – perhaps in an attempt to win an argument with Oxford as to which University was really the older. The northern wing, facing the road, was built during later centuries and has timber-framed brick walls.

In Edwardian times the garden of Merton Hall was in public use as a roller-skating rink.

PLATE 74

NEWNHAM COLLEGE, GATEWAY

One of Cambridge's first colleges for women, Newnham was in the
forefront of the long struggle for equality in education.

Newnham College started small, as a hostel for just five women attending the special "lectures for ladies" that some forward-thinking academics had begun to provide in 1870. It proved popular, and within five years had grown enough to move into its own distinctive "Queen Anne" building – designed by Basil Champneys, who continued to work as the College's architect in the same style for nearly forty years.

Opposition to women's education remained fierce for decades, and would occasionally erupt into physical violence. In 1921 – Newnham's fiftieth anniversary year – the beautiful bronze Pfeiffer Gates which had been installed as a memorial to the first Principal, Anne Jemima Clough, were partly destroyed by a gang of male undergraduates using a handcart as a battering-ram. They were "celebrating" the fact that the University had once again voted against awarding degrees to the women who passed its exams. It would not reverse this decision until 1948.

PLATE 75

THE GRANARY ON THE CAM

The Newnham area, upstream of Queens' College and Silver Street Bridge,
changed a great deal during the late nineteenth century.

The Beales family, who were corn and coal merchants, had already moved their business from the riverside to the railway by 1885, when they sold their house with its adjoining granary to Professor George Darwin (Charles Darwin's son). Darwin and his new wife brought in an architect to transform the buildings into a family home, which they christened Newnham Grange.

Industrial activity was still taking place around them, however. The King's Mill, an imposing four-storey building straddling a pair of water-wheels, would stand across the river from their garden for another forty years – fascinating the four Darwin children, who would watch bags of corn being hauled up via a pulley into the overhanging gable of the mill. Corn was still sometimes delivered by barge, though it arrived more often by horse-drawn waggon.

Newnham Grange was later the first home of New Hall, Cambridge's third women's college, and now forms part of Darwin College, founded in 1964.

PLATE 76

GRANTCHESTER MILL

Grantchester, two miles upstream of the town, was the site of a giant watermill –
similar to Cambridge's King's and Bishop's Mills – which burned down in 1928.

Rupert Brooke, who had lived for a while in "the lovely hamlet Grantchester" where he used to swim naked, accompanied on one memorable occasion by Virginia Woolf, wrote nostalgically in "The Old Vicarage, Grantchester" in 1912:

Oh, is the water sweet and cool,
Gentle and brown, above the pool?
And laughs the immortal river still
Under the mill, under the mill?

The literary and academic associations here are first class. Lord Byron, who studied at Trinity College a hundred years before Brooke enrolled at King's, used to bathe in the same pool – Byron's Pool – just below Grantchester Mill, as, much later, did Ludwig Wittgenstein. Bertrand Russell wrote *Principia Mathematica* while he was living in the Mill House, conveying the heavy manuscripts himself to the University Press in a wheelbarrow.

The idyllic atmosphere of the village and its surrounding fields was celebrated once again during the 1960s by Pink Floyd in "Grantchester Meadows", which is notable for the chorus of birdsong that accompanies the singer's voice.

Grantchester Mill.

PLATE 77

MADINGLEY WINDMILL

At Madingley, just to the west of Cambridge, a hilltop vantage point allows
visitors to appreciate the huge flat expanse of fenland countryside.

The village of Madingley stands on the southern edge of the fens, so its hilltop was an excellent site for a windmill. By the early twentieth century, however, the mill had deteriorated until it was nothing but a picturesque ruin, and it was not destined to survive the Edwardian era. The tenant who lived there, a Mr Charles French, was woken one night in July 1909 by an ominous creaking noise, and shortly afterwards the building collapsed under the weight of the huge millstones, destroying its great oak timbers. The mill was replaced with another post mill, brought from Ellington in the 1930s, which still stands today.

The red-brick buildings of Girton College, visible in the distance, stand in an isolated position on the Huntingdon Road. Locating their pioneering women's college two miles outside Cambridge was a deliberate decision on the part of its founders, who hoped to reassure parents of potential students that the distance would keep their girls safe from the unwelcome attentions of male undergraduates.

Girton College (I)

Cambridge

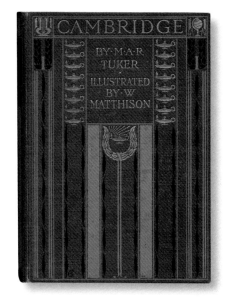

About the Original Book

The commissioning, writing and production of books in A&C Black's *Twenty Shilling Series* was often a fairly swift process: sometimes less than a year from start to finish. *Cambridge* took rather longer, and it can be deduced that the longer gestation was due to one of the publishers' most awkward authors.

Mildred Anna Rosalie Tuker, who was joint author, with her friend Hope Malleson, of *Rome*, published earlier in the same series, was a woman whose name appears only rarely in published reference works but who evidently had a high sense of self-esteem. In late 1904 A&C Black offered her £75 for an unstated number of words, adding that they would pay a ten per cent royalty for every copy that contained the letterpress only, if they published such a volume. Since they never did (and perhaps never intended to), this may be regarded as a clever ploy. Miss Tuker, however, was obviously not satisfied and her fee was increased to £90 in April 1905. This may have been because her text was longer than usual for the series at 85,000 words, though there is no record of whether the publisher was pleased about this: possibly not, since the selling point of these books was the colour plates, and their texts often ran to no more than 40,000 words, just enough to put two pages of text between successive plates. *Cambridge* ran to almost 400 pages, and the charge for corrections to the text ran to 60 per cent of the total setting cost. Since authors were often charged for any corrections above 25 per cent, this must have displeased Adam Black greatly. There is no evidence that Miss Tuker paid the difference.

She made a final attempt at turning the balance in her favour when she asked that the illustrations be grouped together at the back of the book. The request was tersely refused.

On the title page Mildred Tuker is described as "Author of Parts II and III, and joint-author of parts I and IV, of *The Handbooks to Christian and Ecclesiastical Rome*, and Joint Author of *Rome* in this series"; the list of chapters is extensively annotated; there are two pages of bibliography at the front; the captions are fully described on the tissue guards; the text is littered with footnotes; each new subject within a chapter is introduced by a sort of crosshead indented into the text; and there are two extensive indexes. Small wonder that there was a high correction bill for this typesetter's nightmare!

Cambridge was published in a trade edition of 3,000 copies on 3 May 1907. There was, surprisingly, no large-paper limited edition. The book was reprinted only once, in 1912. The fine cover was designed by Carlton Studios, whose monogram can be seen towards the bottom left.

Miss Tuker wrote nothing further for A&C Black, but was more prolific for other publishers. Her work includes *The Past and Future of Ethics* (OUP, 1938), in which she proposes that "man" connote the human race, and "wer" or "werman" be the male person. She spelt the gender "femel" to avoid the suggestion that it is subsidiary to the male. In 1954 her executors gave the Women's Library in east London "a large consignment of material on the position of women".

A New World of Colour Printing

The late Victorians and Edwardians loved colour, and great strides in printing and ink technology allowed them to have it, breaking free of the limitations of the monotone pages of their parents' generation with their woodcuts and steel engravings. Many of these developments came from Germany where, by the turn of the nineteenth century, there was a lucrative industry in colour postcards, greetings cards, and books containing dozens of colour illustrations.

The challenge and promise of colour were quickly taken up in Britain, where presses – especially in London and Edinburgh – started using the latest technology to print colour plates for a range of reference books.

Until the early 1890s, anyone wanting to print a colour image had to design the images in such a way that the different colours, each printed from its own plate, could easily be separated from each other. Many ways were developed to create subtlety in the use of colour, including engraving fine detail into each colour plate, using separate plates for different tones of the same colour, and hand-finishing each plate after it had been printed. Even so, most colour printing in 1900 was fairly crude, and it is clear – especially under the magnifying glass – that the drive for realistic colour still had some way to go.

The best colour printing in 1900, however, was stunning. In the period between 1900 and 1914, before war dried up ink and machinery supplies from

The Old Houses at Bullen, a Jarrold postcard of 1904; a vase of Loughton Hall porcelain, printed in gold and three colours by Bemrose Ltd, from *The Process Year Book* of 1905–6; commercial catalogue illustration printed in three colours, from *The Process Year Book* of 1906–7.

COMMERCIAL CATALOGUE ILLUSTRATION.
Reproduced in three colors direct from the fruit.

"Andsleigh" Color-Tone Process

André & Sleigh, Ltd., London, Liverpool, Glasgow and Paris. Works:—Bushey, Herts.

COLOR SPECIMENS OF ANDRÉ & SLEIGH, LTD., ARE PRINTED IN LORILLEUX & CO.'S INKS.

Carl Hentschel (left) and the original Three Men in a Boat (right) – Carl Hentschel, George Wingrave and Jerome K. Jerome. Hentschel was a good friend of Jerome's.

A portrait study using the three-colour process method (right), from *Penrose's Pictorial Annual* of 1906–7. The Hentschel advertisement (above) was printed in the 1904–5 *Penrose's*. The Chromographoscope (below), invented by du Hauron in 1874, was a dual-purpose machine. It could be used as a camera or as an additive viewer.

Germany to the rest of the world, printing in colour reached a peak not to be reached again until the 1960s.

How did they achieve this quality? It is important to remember that outdoor colour photography as we know it, using colour film to photograph places and people, was not invented until the 1930s. However, from about 1890 onwards, several processes for making colour photographs of inanimate objects in a studio setting were well advanced, and Edwardian photographers were amazingly inventive.

One of the greatest pioneers was a German émigré, Carl Hentschel, who in the 1890s patented the Hentschel Colourtype Process and set up his company in London's Fleet Street. Hentschel developed a massive camera which used three colour filters — red, green and blue — to capture simultaneous images of any flat colour original. At the same time, developments such as the halftone screen, allowing colour gradation to be printed as an almost imperceptible regular pattern of different-sized dots onto paper, was enabling photographed images to be transferred to paper, both in black and white and in the new three-colour "process" method.

It was now possible to photograph flat objects like paintings, or small groups of objects in a studio setting, in colour. And it was possible to use those images, separated into their three component process colours, to print colour images. It was impossible, however, to make colour photographs of the wide outside world, of cities, mountains and crowds of people. Yet once they had seen colour postcards and colour pictures in books, those who could afford to buy such relatively expensive luxuries wanted as much colour as they could get.

The images in this book demonstrate the many ways in which Edwardian inventors, photographers and publishers strove to give their customers what they so craved – the real world on the printed page in full colour.

Sources, Notes and Captions

The images used to complement the paintings come from a wide variety of sources, including books, postcards, museums and libraries. They include photochromes, ephemera, adverts and maps of the period. The photochromes and more than 5,000 others can be seen online at www.ushistoricalarchive. com/photochroms/index.html. The cigarette cards come from a series of 42 cards of Oxford and Cambridge college coats of arms published in 1922. The large coloured numbers refer to the plate numbers.

1 Two views of the Bridge of Sighs. The tinted photograph on the left is from *Pictures in Colour of Cambridge* published by Jarrold and Sons in 1905. On the right is Herbert Railton's illustration from *The Story of Cambridge* by Charles Stubbs, Dean of Ely, also from 1905.

2 The interior sketch by Harry Morley is from *Cambridge from Within* by Charles Tennyson, published by Chatto & Windus in 1913; the main photograph of the Round Church and Union Society is from *Pictures in Colour of Cambridge*. *The Little Hymn Book*, illustrated by Cicely Mary Barker, was published by Blackie in the early 1900s.

3 The photograph (lower left) of Market Hill, *c.*1860, from the corner of Petty Cury, was taken by Arthur Nicholl. The image taken from the opposite side of the market is from *The Cambridge Explorer*, compiled by Hugo Brown publishers with the assistance of the Cambridgeshire Collection. The painting by E.W. Haslehust is from *Cambridge* in the *Beautiful England* series, published by Blackie & Son in 1910.

4 The photograph of the Old Schools gateway, taken before 1889, is from the Cambridge Antiquarian Society (CAS) photographic record. The map from *Story of Cambridge* shows Mill Street and was made by order of Archbishop Parker, while the 1828 engraving of Trinity Lane looking to King's is by H.S. Storer.

5 The main photograph of St John's Street from Trinity, *c.*1890, is from the CAS photographic record. The image on the left is of St John's Street by Harry Morley, dated 1913.

6 The Great Court of Trinity College (left) was published in *Memorials of Cambridge*, issued in parts between 1837 and 1842, and hailed as "decidedly superior to any hitherto published". The main picture is from *Pictures in Colour of Cambridge*. The interior illustration of The Hall is from *Trinity College, Cambridge*, published by Dent in 1906.

7 The photograph of The Spinning House (upper right) is from *The Cambridge Explorer*. Scott & Wilkinson, of Cambridge, took the photograph of St Andrew's Street looking south, decorated for the coronation of King George V in 1911. St Andrew's Street looking north is from the IXL postcard series, *c.*1905.

8 The image of Peterhouse (centre) is from *Pictures in Colour of Cambridge*. The photograph of Emmanuel Church, *c.*1910, comes from *The Cambridge Explorer*. St Peter's College (Peterhouse) is from *Ackermann's Cambridge*.

9 Front court of Peterhouse is a postcard published by Valentine's, one of the most prolific of Edwardian postcard publishers, in 1900.

10 The blocked-up gateway leading to Peterhouse deer park from Coe Fen is a pencil sketch by J. Osbaldeston from 1854. The illustration by H. Toussaint of the Principal Court exterior is from *Cambridge*, by J.W. Clark. The Peterhouse kitchen wall is from *Cambridge* in the *Beautiful England* series published by Blackie & Son, *c.*1910.

11 The lower inset, entitled "Clare Bridge Over Backs", is from *Cambridge: A Sketch Book* by Walter M. Keesey, published by A&C Black in 1913. The upper inset is a postcard from the Valentine's Moonlight Series, postmarked 1903. The main image is an 1890s photochrome.

12 The image on the left of Clare College from the bridge is by Harry Morley, 1913; the postcard is by Valentine's, *c.*1905. The illustration by E.W. Haslehust is from his *Cambridge*.

13 The central image of Latimer is from *Hutchinson's Story of the British Nation*, Vol. 2 (1920), as is that of Latimer preaching before Edward VI.

14 The Trumpington Street view of Pembroke College is from *Pictures in Colour of Cambridge*, while the aerial perspective of Pembroke Hall is from *Ackermann's Cambridge*. The delicate sketch comes from the 1903 edition of *Cambridge and its Story*, published by Dent.

15 The First Court of Pembroke College is from *Pictures in Colour of Cambridge*.

16 The large image of Trinity Hall is from *Ackermann's Cambridge*. The sketch (right) by Herbert Railton and tinted by Fanny Railton is from *Cambridge and its Story*. The interior image of Trinity Hall Library is from *Cambridge* by J.W. Clark, Seeley, 1890.

17 The photograph (bottom right) is by Arthur Nicholls, taken about 1860. The photograph of the horse-drawn tram on the corner of Market Hill, by Percy Salmon, *c.*1900, is from *The Cambridge Explorer*. The centre image of the shop on the corner of Silver Street is by Charles Cudworth.

18 The image of New Court, Corpus Christi, comes from *Pictures in Colour of Cambridge*; the illustration of Old Hall by E.W. Haslehust is from his *Cambridge*.

19 The colour image of St Benedict's Church is from *Pictures in Colour of Cambridge*. The photograph on the left is by W.H. Hayles, and shows buildings in Free School Lane that were removed for the construction of the old Engineering Laboratory in 1893. The 1892 photograph of St Bene't's Church tower is from the CAS photographic survey.

20 The inset shows Harry Morley's 1913 view of King's College. The main picture is a photochrome of King's College from the north.

21 The advertisement for Buol's Café and Restaurant was included in the illustrated supplement to the *Condensed Guide to Cambridge*, 1906. The northward view along King's Parade is from *Pictures in Colour of Cambridge*.

22 The entrance gateway to King's College is from *Pictures in Colour of Cambridge*. *King's College, Cambridge*, by C.R. Fay, was published by Dent in 1907.

23 The plan and the illustration by Edmund H. New of the Chapel and Gibb's Building come from *King's College, Cambridge*. "Young Ballerina Holding a Black Cat", 1895, is by the French painter Pierre Carrier-Belleuse.

24 The centre image of King's College Chapel is from *Ackermann's Cambridge*. The Tudor rose and crown from the chapel interior is from *King's College, Cambridge*.

25 The view from King's Bridge is from *Pictures in Colour of Cambridge*. The inset on the left of King's College Dining Hall from 1908 is from *The Cambridge Explorer*. The inset on the right is a 1910 photograph of E.M. Forster.

26 The great gate of Queen's College and Queen's Lane (left) as seen from St Catharine's is a Valentine's postcard of *c.*1910. The colour image of Queen's College is a photochrome.

27 The centre drawing of The Queen's Gallery is from *Cambridge: A Sketch Book*. The painting of the President's Gallery (right) is an anonymous watercolour dated 1900. Cloisters Court, the left-hand image, is from *Pictures in Colour of Cambridge*.

28 The painting of a punter close to the Mathematical Bridge is by Harry Morley, 1913. The small inset is from *Ackermann's Cambridge*; the main image is an 1890s photochrome.

29 The interior view of St Catharine's College Chapel is from *Ackermann's Cambridge*. Valentine's featured St Catharine's Dining Hall on one of their postcards, as well as the view from Trumpington Street, *c.*1905.

30 The gateway of Jesus College (left) is a Valentine postcard, *c.*1905. Jesus College cloisters and chapel form the focus of the centre image from *Pictures in Colour of Cambridge*. The illustration of Jesus College on the right is from *Ackermann's Cambridge*.

31 Top, a 1908 photograph by Scott and Wilkinson of St Andrew's Street looking to Hobson Street, with the ornate tower of Foster's Bank. The view on the right of Christ's College Gateway is from *Pictures in Colour of Cambridge*, while the image on the left is from *Ackermann's Cambridge*.

32 The cast of the Lady Margaret is from *The Story of Cambridge* published by J.M. Dent in 1905. The image of Charles Darwin is from *Hutchinson's Story of the British Nation*, Vol. 4.

33 Haslehust's leafy illustration of the Fellows' Garden and Pond, Christ's College (centre) is from his *Cambridge*. The mulberry fruit and flowers are from *Familiar Trees*, Vol. 1, published by Cassell in 1906. The portrait of Milton is from *Hutchinson's Story of the British Nation*, published in 1920.

34 The engraving, published by Rock and Co in an 1853 volume entitled *Views of Cambridge*, shows All Saint's Church before it was demolished. Haslehust's painting of the Gateway of St John's (right) is from his *Cambridge*. The view on the left of All Saint's, c.1900, is from *The Cambridge Explorer*. In the centre is a photochrome of St John's.

35 The map of St John's comes from *The Story of Cambridge* by Charles W. Stubbs. The images of the First Court and St John's College Chapel are both from *The Cambridge Explorer*. The 1916 Bamforth hymn postcard features text by Trinity alumnus John Ellerton (1826–63).

36 The central image of the wedding of Charles I and Henrietta Maria in 1625 is from *Hutchinson's Story of the British Nation*, Vol. 2. *Ackermann's Cambridge* is the source of the colour reproduction on the right of St John's Second Court. To the left is an 1890s photochrome.

37 The main illustration is from Vol. 8 of *The London Magazine*, published by Amalgamated Press in 1905. The advertisement for Woodbine cigarettes is from the *Edwardian Scrapbook* based on The Robert Opie Collection, while the illustrated supplement of the *Condensed Guide to Cambridge* is the source of "The Union" Cigar Stores. The portrait of William Wilberforce is from *Hutchinson's Story of the British Nation*, Vol. 3.

38 The Herbert Railton illustration of St John's Library Oriel is from *Cambridge and its Story* by C.W. Stubbs. The E.W. Haslehust painting of the library staircase is from his *Cambridge*.

39 The illustration, entitled "Long Idle Afternoons", is from Vol. 12 of *The London Magazine*, 1910. The 1907 view of St John's Bridge (upper left) is from *The Cambridge Explorer*; the lower left illustration is a photochrome. The advertisement for paper handkerchiefs comes from *Woman at Home*, Vol. 3, published by Warwick Magazine Company in 1910–11.

40 Magdalene College library (bottom right) is from *Ackermann's Cambridge*; the Valentine postcard is c.1905. The portrait of Samuel Pepys is from *Hutchinson's Story of the British Nation*, Vol. 2.

41 Both the main picture (right) and small picture (left) are of Trinity College Great Gate; the former is from *Pictures in Colour of Cambridge*; the latter is a painting by G. Morrow.

42 A picture-postcard view of the Great Court of Trinity College covered in snow, c.1906, and a Valentine Moonlight Series postcard featuring night time at Trinity, c.1903. Upper left is a Haslehust painting of Great Court; the main image is an 1890s photochrome.

43 Wounded soldiers on the grass of Nevile's Court, Trinity, 1915, a photograph by David Moore. The illustration of Nevile's Court with Wren library and the Trinity College plan are from *Trinity College, Cambridge*, Dent, 1906; its decorative cover is also shown here.

44 The drawing of Nevile's Gate, Trinity College, on the left, is from *Trinity College, Cambridge*. At the bottom is a 1910 photograph of Trinity porters from *The Cambridge Explorer*. The colour reproduction of Trinity College Kitchen is from *Ackermann's Cambridge*.

45 The main image and image on the left are from *Pictures in Colour of Cambridge*. During springtime the Backs of the colleges are a mass of flowers, but on 24 April 1908 the snowdrops were covered in snow – postcard from Kidd & Baker.

46 The 1958 photograph by Peter Davey shows the botched attempt by the university Civil Defence team to lower an Austin 7 van to the ground – it had been put there overnight without incident or damage by a group of student engineers. The engraving of Senate House (bottom left) is from the *Condensed Guide to Cambridge*.

47 Three views of the Gate of Virtue, Gonville and Caius College: a 1913 painting by Harry Morley, a 1905 postcard, and an illustration from *Pictures in Colour of Cambridge*.

48 Gonville and Caius College, Gate of Honour, comes from *Cambridge and its Story*. On the right is an illustration by H. Toussaint of the same gate from *Cambridge* by J.W. Clark; the central image is from *Pictures in Colour of Cambridge*.

49 Emmanuel College's Front Court (also known as First Court) with Wren's Chapel flanked on the left by the Hall, in a Valentine's postcard from 1905 (top left), and in *Pictures in Colour of Cambridge*. The inset of Christopher Wren is by Godfrey Kneller.

50 The drawing of Emmanuel College Chapel and Cloisters is by A. Brunet Debaines from *Cambridge* by J.W. Clark. The Harvard shield (right) sits above a nineteenth-century map of Harvard University.

51 The Emmanuel College map comes from the *Condensed Guide to Cambridge*; the view of the college from across the pond is from *The Cambridge Explorer*. The ducks are from a four-colour block print in *Penrose's Pictorial Annual 1907–8*.

52 The picture postcard on the right of Sidney Sussex College was published by Valentine's, c.1905. The image on the left is from *Pictures in Colour of Cambridge*.

53 The view of Downing College with the spire of the Roman Catholic Church in the distance is from *Pictures in Colour of Cambridge*; to the right is a Valentine's postcard of Downing College.

54 The illustration of Pitt Press is from the *Condensed Guide to Cambridge*; the inset of William Pitt the Younger is from *Hutchinson's Story of the British Nation*, Vol. 3. The view along Trumpington Street is from *The Cambridge Explorer*.

55 All the images of the Peas Hill, or Peashill, area of the Market Square are from *The Cambridge Explorer*.

56 On the left is John Maynard Keynes as painted by Roger Eliot Fry. The photograph of David's Bookshop in the 1950s is by John Carter. The photograph of St Edward's Passage during redevelopment was taken by Captain Cyril Hatfield.

57 The photograph of Eaden Lilley's Market Street shop is accompanied by two postcards, one by Judge's (top) c.1910, the other, Valentine's c.1905. The Cadbury's sweet box is from a tri-chromatic reproduction direct from the object by T.G.E. and Co. Ltd, featured in *The Process Year Book* for 1903.

58 The photograph of a female effigy suspended opposite Great St Mary's Church in 1897 is by Cambridge photographer Thomas Stearn. The advertisements for the Blue Boar Hotel and The Café are from the illustrated supplement to the *Condensed Guide to Cambridge*.

59 The view of the Botanic Garden's pond is from *Pictures in Colour of Cambridge*; the inset map is from the *Condensed Guide to Cambridge*.

60 The engraving of 1838 commemorating the coronation of Queen Victoria was lithographed by G. Scharf, Metcalfe & Palmer and reproduced in *Holly Leaves*, 1950. Cambridge Picture Post Card Co. published "Cambridge by Moonlight – Parker's Piece" (top left) around 1905. The Valentine's postcard of 1905 looks towards Parkside. Cricketers on Parker's Piece were featured in *The London Magazine*, Vol. 2, 1902.

61 The swan is a detail of William Etty's painting, "Female Bathers Surprised by a Swan". The 1910 view of Trinity Bridge (right) is from *The Cambridge Explorer*. The view on the left of the same bridge is from a 1907 Valentine's postcard.

62 The main view of the Backs from Trinity Bridge is from *Pictures in Colour of Cambridge*. The inset of Trinity College Library in the 1900s is from *The Cambridge Explorer*.

63 "Pecheur" is a 1907 autochrome photograph from the Ciba Geigy catalogue and published in *The Illustrated History of Colour Photography*, Fountain, 1993. The image of the Old Chesterton Ferry is from *The Cambridge Explorer*.

64 Photographs of the Cambridge Crew of 1910 (left) and the bumps in the 1920s (right) are both from *The Cambridge Explorer*. In the lower right is a drawing of Fen Ditton Church by William West.

65 A version of "The Last of England", painted by Ford Maddox Brown in 1860, is held by the Fitzwilliam Museum. The view of the front of the museum is from *Pictures in Colour of Cambridge*.

66 The inset of Great St Mary's church, engraved by J. Le Keux for *Memorials of Cambridge*, shows the interior before rearrangement in 1863; the main image is from *Pictures in Colour of Cambridge*. The advertisement for E.M. Phillips is from the illustrated supplement to the *Condensed Guide to Cambridge*.

67 At the top, a photograph by Scott & Wilkinson shows the Gordon Highlanders' Band playing on the lawns in front of Addenbrooke's Hospital as part of the Coronation celebrations of 1911. The Valentine's postcard (lower left) shows the frontage of Addenbrooke's Hospital *c*.1905. A Thomas Stearns photograph, "Collecting for the Hospital, Christmas 1906", is shown bottom right.

68 Inset is J.E. Foster's photograph of the quayside from Magdalene Bridge, 1910. The painting by E.W. Haslehust is from his *Cambridge*. The main image of the boathouses and Victoria Bridge is from *Pictures in Colour of Cambridge*.

69 Two panoramic views (left and centre) of Cambridge looking southward from Castle Hill. The first, by William Darton, is dated 1821; the second, by Harry Morley, from 1913. The photochrome on the right is a view from the river looking north towards St John's.

70 Girton College as featured in *Pictures in Colour of Cambridge*. The inset photograph of life at Newnham and Girton, including the "College Fire Brigade", is from the *Penrose Pictorial Annual* of 1909–10. The hockey player is taken from *London Magazine*, Vol. 18, 1907.

71 The map of Robinson Crusoe Island is from *The Story of Cambridge*. The advertisement for Mrs S. Dolby's Boat Houses is the back cover of the *Condensed Guide to Cambridge*. "Cupid Captives" by Gladys M. Baly were depicted in *London Magazine*, Vol. 18, 1907.

72 The centre map shows Mill Street and was made by order of Archbishop Parker; the map on the left features Queen's Lane – both come from *The Story of Cambridge*. The image of Queen's College Gateway is from *The Cambridge Explorer*.

73 "In Full Bloom" is a process colour print from a photograph, from *Penrose's Pictorial Annual 1907–8*. The photograph of Cambridge academics relaxing on the lawns in front of Merton Hall is from the CAS collection. The engraving of the School of Pythagoras by R.B. Harraden in 1809 was published in his *Cantabrigia Depicta* of 1811.

74 The main image of the "Three Halls" of Newnham College is from *Pictures in Colour of Cambridge*. Two ladies in academic dress is a *carte de visite* by Cambridge photographer Ralph Starr, *c*.1890. The two lower photographs of the college (right) and the gateway (left) are from *The Cambridge Explorer*.

75 The main view of King's Mill is from *Pictures in Colour of Cambridge*. The photograph of Darwin's House from Queens College dating from about 1895 (inset left) is from the CAS collection. "The King's and Bishop's Mill" (inset right), was painted by R.B. Harraden, *c*.1800.

76 The small photograph of Grantchester Mill after the fire of 1928 was taken by Ted Mott. Grantchester Mill from the millpool (main image) as known by Rupert Brooke is from a Frith postcard. On the left, Haslehust's painting of Grantchester millpool is from *Pictures in Colour of Cambridge*.

77 "Windmills on the Thurne, Norfolk", by Alfred Heaton Cooper, is from *Norfolk and Suffolk* published by A&C Black in 1921. The inset of Madingley Windmill is a 1904 postcard from a photograph by E.C. Hoppett. The postcard of Girton College is from *The Cambridge Explorer*.

After Many Years, W.E. Heitland, CUP, 1926.
The Architectural History of the University of Cambridge, R. Willis and J.W. Clark, CUP, 1886.
As I Remember, E.E.C. Jones, A&C Black, 1922.
The Bright Countenance, Hodder and Stoughton, 1957.
Cambridge, Noel Barwell, Blackie, 1910.
Cambridge, A. Gray, Methuen, 1912.
Cambridge, Frank Reeve, Batsford, 1976.
Cambridge: A Brief Study in Social Questions, E. Jebb, Macmillan and Bowes, 1906.
Cambridge, A Concise Guide, J.W. Clark, Macmillan and Bowes, 1902.
Cambridge: A Sketch Book, W.M. Keesey, A&C Black, 1913.
Cambridge and its Story, C.W. Stubbs, Dent, 1903.
The Cambridge Annual, 1905–1906, Cambridge Express, 1906.
Cambridge Commemorated, L. and H. Fowler, CUP, 1984.
Cambridge from Within, C. Tennyson, Chatto and Windus, 1913.
Cambridge, The Hidden History, Alison Taylor, Tempus, 1999.
Cambridge Revisited, A.B. Gray, Heffer, 1921.
Cambridge: The Shaping of a City, Peter Bryan, Bryan, 1999.
The Cantab, Shane Leslie, Chatto and Windus, 1926.
A Concise History of the University of Cambridge, Elisabeth Leedham-Green, CUP, 1996.
Desirable Young Men, Patrick Carleton, Philip Allan, 1932.
Emily Davies and Girton College, B.N. Stephen, Constable, 1927.
The Film of Memory, Shane Leslie, Michael Joseph, 1938.
Francis Jenkinson, University Librarian, H.F. Stewart, CUP, 1926.
The Granta and its Contributors 1889–1914, F.A. Rice, Constable, 1924.
Henry Jackson: A Memoir, R. St John Parry, CUP, 1926.
Highways and Byways in Cambridge and Ely, J.W. Conybeare, Macmillan, 1910.
A History of the University of Cambridge, Vol. 4: 1870–1990, Christopher Brooke, CUP, 1993.
The Housing of Cambridge, Henry Cayley, Rivington, 1904.
Images of Cambridge, Mike Petty, Breedon, 2006.
Kett of Cambridge: An Eminent Victorian and His Family, Anna de Salvo, National Extension College, 1993.
Leaves from a Cambridge Notebook, O.J. Dunlop, Simpkin Marshall, 1907.
The Longest Journey, E.M. Forster, Blackwood, 1907.
Memories of Henry Arthur Morgan, Master of Jesus College 1885–1912, I.L. Morgan, Hodder and Stoughton, 1927.
Period Piece, Gwen Raverat, Faber, 1952.
The Romance of the Cambridge Colleges, F. Gribble, Mills and Boon, 1913.
Town and Gown, Rowland Parker, Patrick Stephens, 1983.
Vanishing Cambridgeshire, Mike Petty, Breedon, 2006.
Victorian Eton and Cambridge, W.E. Wortham, Barker, 1956.
William Heffer, 1843–1928, Sidney Heffer, Heffer, 1952.
Wittgenstein: A Life, Brian McGuiness. Duckworth, 1988.

The Times Past Archive

The *Memories of Times Past* series would be inconceivable without the massive Times Past Archive, a treasury of books, magazines, atlases, postcards and printed ephemera from the "golden age" of colour printing between 1895 and 1915.

From the time several years ago when the project was first conceived, the collecting of material from all over the world has proceeded in earnest. As well as a complete set of the 92 A&C Black 20 *Shilling* colour books, which are the inspiration for the series, the Archive houses full sets of period *Baedeker* and *Murray's Guides*, almost every colour-illustrated travel book from illustrious publishing houses like Dent, Jack, Cassell, Blackie and Chatto & Windus, and a massive collection of reference works with colour plates on subjects from railways and military uniforms to wild flowers and birds' eggs.

The Archive also contains complete runs of all the important periodicals of the time that contained colour illustrations, including the pioneering *Penrose's Pictorial Annual: An Illustrated Review of the Graphic Arts*; the first-ever British colour magazine, *Colour*; ladies' magazines like *Ladies' Field* and *The Crown*; and more popular titles like *The Connoisseur* and *The London Magazine*.

These years were vintage years for atlas publishing, and the Times Past Archive contains such gems as Keith Johnston's *Royal Atlas of Modern Geography*, *The Harmsworth Atlas*, Bartholomew's *Survey Atlas of England and Wales*, and the *Illustrated and Descriptive Atlas of The British Empire*.

Last but not least, the Archive includes a wealth of smaller items – souvenirs, postcards, tickets, programmes, catalogues, posters, and all the colourful ephemera with which the readers of the original 20 *Shilling* books would have been familiar.

The Times Past Website

The website to accompany this project can be found at www. memoriesoftimespast.com, where you will find further information about the birth and development of the project, together with the complete original texts of titles published to date. There is also an area where you can take part in discussions raised by readers of the books who want to take their interest further and share their memories and passions with others. The website will start small and elegant, as you would expect of an "Edwardian website", but it will gradually become what you and we together make it, a place for devotees of art and culture from a century ago to meet and be inspired.

Every effort has been made to ensure the accuracy of the information presented in this book. The publisher will not assume liability for damages caused by inaccuracies in the data and makes no warranty whatsoever expressed or implied. The publisher welcomes comments and corrections from readers, which will be incorporated in future editions. Please email corrections@memoriesoftimespast.com

Acknowledgements

Derek Stubbings
John Durrant
Allan Brigham
Mick le Moignan, Derrin Mappledoram and Peter Davey for the Austin 7 photograph accompanying Plate 46.
Glynn Waite, and the Transport History Collection at Brunel University, for images of period railway tickets.

Many of the early postcards and photographs included in this book have been collected by Hugo Brown in association with The Cambridge Collection on a CD, *The Cambridge Explorer CD-ROM*. More information about this publication, together with ordering information, can be found at www. cambridge-explorer.org.uk

Market Hill, Cambridge by Grace Golden, *Recording Britain*, Vol II, OUP, 1947.